Creating Effective TEAMS

FIFTH EDITION

Creating Effective TEAMS

A Guide for Members and Leaders

FIFTH EDITION

Susan A. Wheelan

G.D.Q Associates, Inc.

Los Angeles | London | New Delhi
Singapore | Washington DC

Los Angeles | London | New Delhi
Singapore | Washington DC

FOR INFORMATION:

SAGE Publications, Inc.
2455 Teller Road
Thousand Oaks, California 91320
E-mail: order@sagepub.com

SAGE Publications Ltd.
1 Oliver's Yard
55 City Road
London, EC1Y 1SP
United Kingdom

SAGE Publications India Pvt. Ltd.
B 1/I 1 Mohan Cooperative Industrial Area
Mathura Road, New Delhi 110 044
India

SAGE Publications Asia-Pacific Pte. Ltd.
3 Church Street
#10-04 Samsung Hub
Singapore 049483

Printed in the United States of America

Library of Congress Cataloging-in-Publication Data

Wheelan, Susan A.
Creating effective teams : a guide for members and leaders / Susan A. Wheelan, G.D.Q. Associates, Inc.— Fifth Edition.

pages cm

ISBN 978-1-4833-4612-0 (pbk.)

1. Teams in the workplace. I. Title.

HD66.W485 2015
658.4′022—dc23   2014024362

This book is printed on acid-free paper.

Acquisitions Editor: Maggie Stanley
Editorial Assistant: Nicole Mangona
Production Editor: Kelly DeRosa
Copy Editor: Rachel Keith
Typesetter: C&M Digitals (P) Ltd.
Proofreader: Sue Irwin
Indexer: Scott Smiley
Cover Designer: Dally Verghese
Marketing Manager: Liz Thornton

Certified Chain of Custody
SUSTAINABLE FORESTRY INITIATIVE
Promoting Sustainable Forestry
www.sfiprogram.org
SFI-01268

SFI label applies to text stock

14 15 16 17 18 10 9 8 7 6 5 4 3 2 1

BRIEF CONTENTS

Preface		x
About the Author		xii
1.	Why Groups?	1
2.	Effective Organizational Support for Teams	7
3.	From Groups to Teams: The Stages of Group Development	24
4.	How Do High Performance Teams Function?	36
5.	Effective Team Members	49
6.	Effective Team Leadership	70
7.	Navigating Stage 1	90
8.	Surviving Stage 2	96
9.	Reorganizing at Stage 3	108
10.	Sustaining High Performance	114
11.	Virtual Teams	125
12.	Recent Research	130
References		137
Bibliography		138
Index		151

DETAILED CONTENTS

—◆◆◆—

Preface   x

About the Author   xii

1. Why Groups?   1
    Groups Have a Long History of Success   1
    We Need Groups Every Day   1
    Groups Increase Our Knowledge Base   2
    When Teams Are Good, They're Very, Very Good   2
    Creating Effective Teams   3
    How to Use This Book   5

2. Effective Organizational Support for Teams   7
    Plant Groups in a Favorable Organizational Climate   7
    Give Groups What They Need to Do Their Best   11
    Pick Members Based on Their Ability to Do the Task and
        Their Ability to Contribute to Group Success   13
    Educate People for Group Participation Competence   14
    Avoid Unsubstantiated Team Development and Consultation
        Strategies   15
    Avoid Helping Groups Too Much   16
    Make Sure That Each Group Has Enough Autonomy
        to Do Its Work but Remains Connected With the
        Rest of the Organization   17
    Conduct Organizational Support Reviews Regularly   17

    THE ORGANIZATIONAL SUPPORT CHECKLIST   18

**3. From Groups to Teams: The Stages of
Group Development**   24
    Stage 1: Dependency and Inclusion   25
    Stage 2: Counterdependency and Fighting   26

Stage 3: Trust and Structure 27
Stage 4: Work 28
Surviving Group Development 30

4. How Do High Performance Teams Function? **36**
The Characteristics of High Performance Teams 36
10 Keys to Productivity 37
Goals 38
Roles 39
Interdependence 40
Leadership 41
Communication and Feedback 42
Discussion, Decision Making, and Planning 43
Implementation and Evaluation 43
Norms and Individual Differences 43
Structure 44
Cooperation and Conflict Management 45

TEAM PERFORMANCE CHECKLIST 46

5. Effective Team Members **49**
Don't Blame Others for Group Problems 50
Encourage the Process of Goal, Role, and Task Clarification 53
Encourage the Adoption of an Open Communication
    Structure in Which All Member Input and
    Feedback Is Heard 54
Promote an Appropriate Ratio of Task Communications
    to Supportive Communications 56
Promote the Use of Effective Problem-Solving and
    Decision-Making Procedures 56
Encourage the Establishment of Norms That Support
    Productivity, Innovation, and Freedom of Expression 59
Go Along With Norms That Promote Group Effectiveness
    and Productivity 60
Promote Group Cohesion and Cooperation 61

EFFECTIVE MEMBER CHECKLIST 64

6. Effective Team Leadership **70**
Don't Take On Every Leadership Assignment
    You Are Offered 72
Adjust Your Leadership Style to Meet the Developmental
    Needs of the Group at a Particular Time 73

Leadership at Stage 1: Be a Directive and Confident Leader   74
Leadership at Stage 2: When Members Begin to
   Demand More Participation in Running the Group,
   Slowly Begin to Empower Them   77
Leadership at Stage 3: Involve Members in the
   Leadership Function   81
Leadership at Stage 4: Participate as an Expert Member
   of Your Team   83

EFFECTIVE LEADER CHECKLIST   84

7. Navigating Stage 1   **90**
   Goals of Stage 1   90
   Concerns About Safety and Inclusion   91
   Dependency on the Designated Leader   92
   A Wish for Order and Structure   93

8. Surviving Stage 2   **96**
   Goals of Stage 2   96
   Creating a Unified Group Culture   97
   Creating a Unified and Effective Group Structure   102

9. Reorganizing at Stage 3   **108**
   Goals of Stage 3   108
   Fine-Tuning Roles, Organization, and Procedures   108
   Solidifying Positive Relationships   111

10. Sustaining High Performance   **114**
   Goals of Stage 4   114
   Getting the Work Done Well   115
   Making Decisions   117
   Cohesion and Conflict   119
   Maintaining High Performance   121

11. Virtual Teams   **125**
   Video Conferences   126
   LinkedIn   127
   Skype   127
   Blogging   128
   Virtual GDQ Online Scoring Systems   128
   Star Trek Changed the World   129

12. Recent Research   **130**
   On Average, How Long Does the Development
   Process Take?   130

Does Group Size Affect Group Productivity? 131
Does Group Age in Months Affect Group Productivity? 132
How Do Work Groups in Different Sectors Function? 132
Do Leadership Teams or Membership Work Teams
    Function More Effectively? 135
A Final Thought 136

References **137**

Bibliography **138**

Index **151**

PREFACE

Over the 15 years since the publication of the first edition of *Creating Effective Teams*, work group research and methods to improve work groups have continued to develop. Also, because work team members and leaders frequently operate internationally, the world has become more connected. I wrote this fifth edition to keep up to date with new information, such as recent changes in work group research and the way virtual teams operate.

It is my hope that academics, human resource managers, educators, organizational consultants, health care managers, business teams, and others will find this edition helpful and interesting.

Acknowledgments

SAGE Publications would like to thank the following reviewers:

Stephen R. Balzac
Wentworth Institute of Technology

David Biemer
Texas State University

David S. Bright
Wright State University

Denise M. Cumberland
University of Louisville

Gloria J. Galanes
Missouri State University

Carol Schmer
University of Missouri, Kansas City

Jeff Zimmerman
Northern Kentucky University

ABOUT THE AUTHOR

———•◆•———

Susan A. Wheelan is president of G.D.Q Associates, Inc. Until 2001, she was a professor of psychological studies and faculty director of the Training and Development Center at Temple University. Dr. Wheelan received Temple University's Great Teacher Award in 1992. She has also worked as a psychologist in a number of hospital and clinical settings. Currently, Dr. Wheelan is engaged in research projects and consults with work groups in the United States and Europe.

Dr. Wheelan is the author of *Facilitating Training Groups*; *Group Processes: A Developmental Perspective*; *Creating Effective Teams: A Guide for Members and Leaders*; and *Faculty Groups: From Frustration to Collaboration*. She is editor of the *Handbook of Group Research and Practice* and co-editor of *The Lewin Legacy: Field Theory in Current Practice and Advances in Field Theory*. She has also written 66 research articles for publication.

ONE

WHY GROUPS?

Groups Have a Long History of Success

People have formed work groups to accomplish goals and tasks since the beginning of human history. The small group, whose members work collaboratively for their mutual benefit or survival, is the oldest form of social organization. Groups have played a major role in both the survival of human beings and the development of human culture. Some would argue that our ability to work together was, and is, the key to human survival and advancement. Work groups have a long and remarkable track record of success. From the beginning of human history, people have used work groups to generate new ideas, get things done, and nurture individuals.

We Need Groups Every Day

Most people participate in work groups on a daily basis and have always done so. Imagine building a house or an airplane, putting out a newspaper, developing a strategic plan, or doing almost anything, all by yourself. Of course, there are tasks that can, or should, be done by one person, but given the complex nature of work in the 21st century, more and more tasks require people to work in groups.

There was a time when people tried to get rid of the collaborative nature of work. We set up assembly lines and precisely defined each person's job so that he or she could do that job without input from others. Often, this was effective. The industrial revolution was a success, after all. But this strategy worked best for repetitive tasks in which innovation, creativity, and problem solving were not necessary. In the 21st century, few such tasks are performed by humans. Robots have most of those jobs.

Even in the early industrial period there were groups throughout the workplace. People made decisions together. Engineers created new products together. Managers determined schedules and hammered out work flow processes together. There was a need for work groups then, and there is an even greater need for work groups now.

Groups Increase Our Knowledge Base

The current emphasis on work groups reflects our growing awareness that the complexity of work at this point in history necessitates collaboration. More work is conducted by groups of employees than by individuals because collaboration is the only way to accomplish complex tasks. Too much knowledge and too many different skills are needed for any individual to accomplish such tasks alone.

The knowledge explosion led us to reevaluate the way we work. The assembly line model has lost much of its relevance. The individual contributor no longer can go it alone. Teamwork is necessary for organizational success.

When Teams Are Good, They're Very, Very Good

Lots of people don't like to work in groups. Many of us don't like to go to meetings and think they're a waste of time. Most of us have had bad experiences working in groups. Some of us associate work groups with fighting, hurt feelings, and inefficiency. This is not surprising, because many groups have difficulty functioning effectively. Even groups that ultimately succeed in becoming teams have periods that are stressful and unpleasant.

The distinction between a work group and a team is an important one in this book. A work group is composed of members who are striving to create a shared view of goals and to develop an efficient and effective organizational structure in which to accomplish those goals. A work group becomes a team when shared goals have been established and effective methods to accomplish those goals are in place. How work groups become teams is what this book is about. It chronicles how some groups develop into high performance teams and why other groups fail to become teams. Throughout the book, I refer both to groups that have not reached a level of effectiveness and productivity as work groups and to groups that are effective and productive as teams.

When a group becomes a team, there is nothing like it. Work doesn't feel like a chore. It's fun. Members of high performance teams feel involved, committed, and valued. Time flies, work flows, and people help each other to meet goals and deadlines. There's nothing like playing on a winning team. Effective teams are more productive, and that means that companies and organizations win, too. The trick to creating teams is to learn enough about how work groups function that we can increase the chances that they will become high performance teams.

Creating Effective Teams

Books, articles, and research studies that attempt to describe the characteristics of high performance work teams have proliferated over the past few decades. The importance of teamwork in increasing organizational productivity is clear, and everyone has jumped on the bandwagon to ensure team success. However, in recent years, there has been a significant decrease in methods used to improve team performance. Instead of consulting with team members and leaders together, many trainers and consultants focus on coaching leaders. The assumption is that leaders who are coached will be able to lead group members to high performance. I have yet to find any solid research to support this assumption. Members and leaders need to know how work groups develop across time. They need to know what members and leaders should do to help their group become a high performance team.

Groups and teams have always been with us, and the importance of teams in the workplace is here to stay. Despite the intense focus on coaching leaders, strategies designed to increase work group effectiveness continue to exist. Unfortunately, current team development strategies range from the ridiculous to the sublime. (My personal favorite in the ridiculous category is a group of executives playing basketball while riding donkeys as a way to build a high

> ### Box 1.1   Corporate Teams at Higher Stages of Development
>
> At higher stages of development, corporate teams:
>
> - Are rated higher in customer service
>
> - Take less time to complete work
>
> - Generate more revenue for the corporation

performance team. Second best goes to a group of accountants who took cooking lessons with a very pricey chef in order to improve their team meetings at work.) As a result of the multitude of available strategies, determining what to do to help groups perform effectively has become extremely difficult and has spurred questions such as, "Which strategies work? Which strategies are based on solid research evidence? Which strategies are least time-consuming and most cost-effective?" These and similar questions are on the minds of many people charged with ensuring the effectiveness of organizational work groups. Until recently, however, answers to these questions were not so easy to come by. The good news about this intense focus on groups is that it has rejuvenated the scientific study of work groups and high performance teams and made the answers to these questions easier to obtain.

We don't yet know everything there is to know about groups, but we know enough to be able to help people working in groups. We know enough to answer the difficult questions posed earlier. That's what this book is about. The goal of *Creating Effective Teams* is to translate what we've learned about groups and teams into straightforward, user-friendly, practical guidelines for members and leaders. This book will also provide guidance for those who interact with a particular work group and for those who manage work groups.

I bring about 40 years of experience with groups and teams to this project, and I'm not bored yet. Studying groups and working with their members and leaders is endlessly fascinating and challenging. Beyond that, I believe that helping work groups to become high performance teams is crucial not only to the bottom line but also to the creation of humane, interesting, diverse, and challenging workplaces. I hope this book continues the work of the first four editions in furthering the achievement of those goals.

How to Use This Book

Originally, this book grew out of a number of requests I'd had from organizational members to write a jargon-free how-to book describing how work groups function and what to do to help work groups become high performance teams. Although I was not enamored of how-to books, I decided to try my hand at this one because the topic is so important. My decision turned out to be a good one. *Creating Effective Teams* has been read by thousands of team members and leaders, in a number of countries, and by team consultants charged with helping groups become high performance teams. I wrote this fifth edition to keep the ball rolling and to add new information that has emerged since the fourth edition was published.

As in the first four editions, whatever I write is based on research evidence, and if I'm speculating, I'll let you know. I promise not to overwhelm you with references in the text; those references will appear at the end of the book. If you want more information, the references will be there for you. In fact, in response to requests from readers, I have included more references and recent studies.

I've included recent research throughout the book and a few things I've heard, witnessed, been told about, or asked people about over the years. These will appear in boxes like the one in this chapter. These anecdotes have helped me, and people I've worked with, to maintain a sense of humor and compassion about working in groups and teams. I hope you find them useful.

This book is meant to be used, not just read. Members of newly formed groups could begin by reading the first six chapters and discussing them together as a way of getting off to a good start. Chapter 2 describes what the larger organization can do to help groups be successful. Chapter 3 discusses how groups develop and function. Chapter 4 outlines the characteristics of productive teams, which will help members of a new group know what they're shooting for. Chapters 5 and 6 describe the characteristics of effective members and effective leaders, respectively.

Talk with each other about what you've read. Use the information as a way to begin to organize your group. Use the book as you would use a manual for a computer program. When you get stuck, refer to the appropriate chapter. There are a few checklists scattered throughout the book. Use the checklists to monitor your group's progress.

Once the group gets under way, refer to Chapter 7, which describes typical situations that arise in Stage 1 of group development, outlining ways in which members and leaders can be helpful during this stage. Chapters 8 and 9 do the same thing for groups at Stage 2 and Stage 3, respectively. Chapter 10 outlines how to reach and sustain high performance at Stage 4. I have added two additional chapters that have been requested by readers: The topic of Chapter 11 is virtual teams, and Chapter 12 covers recent research related to work teams.

Reading this book once won't be enough. Like other changes in attitudes or behavior, learning to apply this information in the work groups you belong to will take time. Attitudes and behaviors don't change overnight. If you read and work with this information, however, it will happen. And you, like others before you, will find your work groups transformed into high performance teams.

TWO

EFFECTIVE ORGANIZATIONAL SUPPORT FOR TEAMS

━━━◆◆◆━━━

S ome organizations have been very successful in making the shift to a team environment. Others haven't done so well. There is a compelling reason for organizations to help work groups to become effective, however. Based on my assessments of more than 700 work groups whose members had been working together for six months or more, only 46% of those groups were capable of contributing to their organization's goals; 54% were not. Of the 700 work groups, only 17% were high performance teams. Although organizational support is not the only thing that work groups need, it plays a key role.

This chapter outlines what research and theory teach us about the role of the organization in facilitating or inhibiting the development of high performance work teams. That role is quite large and very important, but it receives little organizational attention. The reason for this is simple: It is easier to create work groups and focus our efforts on group results than it is to address organizational issues that may be inhibiting group performance. If organizations want effective teams, however, all organization members, especially upper management, should consider using the following guidelines for creating them.

Plant Groups in a Favorable Organizational Climate

Work groups and teams function better in an organizational culture that encourages high performance by following these principles:

- Clearly define the organization's mission
- Support innovation

- Expect success
- Value superior quality and service
- Pay attention to detail
- Value team recommendations
- Set clear expectations for group output, quality, timing, and pacing
- Reward teamwork rather than individual performance

I discuss each of these principles in more detail in this section.

Clearly Define the Organization's Mission

Groups flourish when their members are clear about what business they are in. This may seem obvious, but it is not always so. Once, when I asked a group what the mission of its organization was, the members couldn't tell me even though the organization's mission statement was clearly displayed on the wall of the group's meeting room. In another case, I asked a group what its organization's mission was, and the members sang the mission statement. Their singing was not sweet or lyrical, but done in a singsong manner expressing derision and disrespect. Not only do organization members need to know the words contained in the mission statement, but they also need to understand and believe those words.

Support Innovation

Some organizations tend to do things the way they've always been done. In organizations where this is the case, or where organization members believe it is the case, groups will have more difficulty being successful. Putting people together as a group, and thus combining their intelligence and creativity, often leads members to come up with new and unexpected ideas and solutions. If the group is functioning in an organization that encourages new ideas and new ways of doing things, group members feel energized and supported. If not, group members quickly become dispirited and begin to believe that there is no point in making suggestions that challenge the status quo.

Expect Success

Some organizations don't expect to be successful. This may sound absurd, but there are many different ways in which this attitude is expressed by organization members. Here are just a few examples:

"What do you expect? This is a government agency."

"The CEO is leaving soon and doesn't really care about what we do."

"We're going to be merged anyway."

"People would rather be safe than successful."

If attitudes such as these exist in an organizational culture, group members will not give their best effort because they believe that giving 100% is not encouraged or valued.

Value Superior Quality and Service

In the real world, there is always some tension among quality, service, and profit. However, if organization members perceive that profit is more important than quality and service, they will become dispirited and cynical. Here are some examples of how this is expressed:

"People care more about their stock options than doing a good job."

"They want us to pretend to be working to keep the inspectors off our backs."

"They talk about customer service, but they don't really mean it."

Pay Attention to Detail

"Get a group together and work out this policy issue" is an example of a directive from upper management that has no detail and leaves the group leader with little to go on. A better alternative would be for management to give the group leader a clear definition of the group's task, supply all backup materials, and provide awareness of and planning regarding group membership, time lines, meeting times, workloads, availability of potential members, and the like.

Value Team Recommendations

If group members believe that whatever they come up with will be rejected or changed by upper management, the chances of group success are diminished. If group leaders are told in advance what the group should come up with, success is even more unlikely. Again, this is self-evident, but, unfortunately, examples such as these are all too common. In an environment where team recommendations are not valued, it is clear to all that groups are used to make the organization seem to be seeking group input when, in fact, it is not.

Set Clear Expectations for Group Output, Quality, Timing, and Pacing

If the group is given realistic guidelines and goals for what members are expected to produce and by when, the chances of success are much higher. For example, it is unrealistic to give a group two months to complete a complex task, especially if the members of that group have not worked together as a group in the past. It is also unrealistic to give a group a long-term project without some way of measuring progress along the way.

Reward Teamwork Rather Than Individual Performance

How to reward teamwork rather than individual performance is one of the most difficult issues that organizations face with regard to setting up work groups. Most compensation systems are designed to evaluate and reward individual contributions, not team contributions. If individuals are to be motivated to create a high performance team, however, then the team's performance should be a determinant of compensation and bonuses.

Team compensation systems are discussed and written about quite a lot. However, most organizations still don't have team compensation systems in place. When the first four editions of *Creating Effective Teams* were published, few team compensation systems were available. That is no longer the case. Despite the availability of these models, however, many organizations still have not made the shift to team compensation.

Some organizations use recognition of team performance as a substitute for financial reward. Although this is helpful in some cases, this type of recognition has to be thought out carefully. Sometimes recognition of one team may create competition between teams. This can inhibit performance, because most teams rely on cooperation from other teams to accomplish their goals. In other cases, certain kinds of recognition may be a source of embarrassment to some team members.

Successful team compensation strategies are now readily available. Ideally, employees will be compensated both for meeting their individual goals and for their membership on a team that has met its goals and objectives. Organizations that don't offer this combination will not get maximum results from their teams.

Give Groups What They Need to Do Their Best

Work groups function better in organizations that:

- Establish meaningful group goals and tasks that are varied and require skill and interdependence
- Establish meaningful group goals and tasks that require continuous learning
- Establish access to the human resources necessary to accomplish group goals
- Establish access to the technical resources necessary to accomplish tasks
- Establish defined team work areas

Establish Meaningful Group Goals and Tasks That Are Varied and Require Skill and Interdependence

Group members function better when they feel that group goals and tasks are meaningful and interesting and challenge them to think and work to capacity. If tasks are seen as routine or boring, motivation is diminished. Of course, many organizational tasks are routine or boring but must nevertheless be done. A team format may not be the best way to accomplish those tasks.

Group goals and tasks should also require interdependence. That is, a team should be necessary to accomplish them. Again, this seems self-evident, but the following examples will make it obvious that many groups have goals and tasks that do not require members to work together. These groups are treated as teams when in fact they are not teams:

- Phone solicitors who work independently but are called a team and meet once a week to discuss team performance
- Salespeople who work independently, are paid for individual sales, and meet once a month to discuss team performance
- The top 50 administrators in an organization, who meet monthly to hear a report from the CEO
- People who report to the same boss but don't interact with each other at any other time

Establish Meaningful Group Goals and Tasks That Require Continuous Learning

Groups with goals and tasks that require continuous learning are the most successful groups. In fact, the best thing about a group with such goals and tasks is that its members will learn from each other and will seek out information to learn more about how to proceed. If a group's goals and tasks don't require new learning, a group format is probably not necessary for their accomplishment. Give group members the tools they need to be successful.

Establish Access to the Human Resources Necessary to Accomplish Group Goals

A group that is expected to produce a new product on time and under budget but has no authority over or access to the people who set production schedules will not be successful. A group that is expected to determine best practices in a certain area but has no budget to visit other organizations or to consult experts in that area will probably be unsuccessful. A group that is mired in conflict and cannot ask for assistance from an internal or external consultant to help its members work out their differences will also have great difficulty being successful. Make sure that team members have the help they need.

Box 2.1   Old English

The boss asked, "What are you guys going to need to do your best work?" A team member replied, "A work space with more modern equipment than Dickens used would be helpful."

Establish Access to the Technical Resources Necessary to Accomplish Tasks

You can't build a house without tools. However, some teams I've worked with have been expected to accomplish tasks without even minimal access to computer equipment, fax machines, computer programs, archival materials, and other resources necessary for goal achievement.

Establish Defined Team Work Areas

A group needs a territory. This had been difficult for larger organizations whose group members are spread out over large geographic areas. In earlier editions of *Creating Effective Teams*, I said that "while e-mail and teleconferencing can help to some extent, groups do better when they have regular face-to-face meetings." I have softened my opinion on this in the last few years. We have become used to conference calls, video conferencing, group discussions via e-mail, and Skype. Some research in this area suggests that these forms of work group interaction can work well. I still advocate periodic face-to-face meetings. If distance prohibits frequent meetings, the meetings that do occur should be long enough to allow extended planning, discussion, and decision making. For groups in the same location, a defined work area is very useful. Proximity makes communication easier and allows the work to progress faster. After all, we are still human. We need to know the people in our groups. We don't need to know other members intimately, but we do need to know people's thoughts and attitudes about the work we're doing together.

Pick Members Based on Their Ability to Do the Task and Their Ability to Contribute to Group Success

A lot more research has been done about leaders than about members. Thousands of studies have been done to determine what makes a good group leader. Even with all the attention paid to leadership, we still don't know very much. In the case of members, we know even less.

What is known about effective members is discussed in more detail in Chapter 5. As a preview, however, I can say that the research literature does not conclude that personality assessment of potential group members or the personality or style compatibility of group members is key to group success. Rather, it suggests that the best work groups comprise members who are knowledgeable about how groups operate and about the group's tasks.

In addition, the research literature does not suggest that group members have to like each other or socialize outside work for their groups to be successful. Instead, it suggests that people trained in the technical aspects of the job, in how groups function, and in what members and leaders can do to help the group function more effectively make good group members.

Educate People for Group Participation Competence

Organizations that focus on educating and training people about the technical aspects of their jobs and about effective group participation will increase the likelihood that their groups will become high performance teams.

Most organizations do a reasonable job of choosing people with technical expertise and providing ongoing technical training to their employees. When it comes to facilitating the group participation of members or leaders, however, organizations don't do so well. Most employees in large organizations have attended the obligatory half-day workshop on group dynamics, and many have attended leadership training or team development workshops. However, the quality and duration of these experiences vary widely.

Imagine providing computer training that is inaccurate or incomplete. Imagine giving technicians inexact information about turbine maintenance. Although I'm sure that this happens occasionally, organizations tend to be careful and conservative about technical training. Unfortunately, this is not the case with group or leadership training.

Box 2.2   Looking Good

As part of a class assignment, some of my students surveyed companies, asking how they selected outside trainers to conduct team-building workshops. The most common response was that the trainer's brochure and materials (e.g., overhead, manuals) had to be of the highest professional quality. The trainer's references were rarely checked.

Organizations often forget to ask training providers some very basic and important questions. These questions include the following:

- What is taught in this training?
- Is the content of the training based on solid research evidence?
- Can the trainer provide social science references that support the training content?
- Does the training work? Do people who attend this training actually perform better as group members or leaders?

These questions do not have easy answers, and training providers should not be expected to be able to answer each question completely. All training providers should be able to answer the first three pretty well, however. Trainers should be aware of the body of literature that supports the content of the training they provide. Trainers should also be aware of literature that disagrees with their approach. If a trainer is unable to answer the first three questions, head for the hills.

With regard to the fourth question, we know that most approaches to team-building training have little or no effect. People who attend group dynamics or leadership training do not necessarily perform better as group members or leaders. This is because individuals rather than work groups are trained. More effective approaches are described in the next section.

Avoid Unsubstantiated Team Development and Consultation Strategies

Because not all work groups manage to reach high levels of effectiveness and productivity on their own, efforts to develop intervention strategies that will assist groups in meeting goals and maximizing effectiveness have been used for many years. Unfortunately, most team interventions don't work. For example, Sundstrom, DeMeuse, and Futrell (1990) examined a number of intervention studies and noted that four of the nine interventions had positive effects on group performance. That means that for five of the nine, performance was unchanged. Interventions have had mixed results, at best, on group effectiveness and productivity.

Guzzo, Jett, and Katzell (1985) conducted an analysis of 330 group intervention studies. They found that interventions that included goal setting and feedback had the most positive effects on group productivity. Interventions that take group development into account are also useful, because groups need different types of interventions at different points in their development.

To date, the most promising intervention type appears to be goal setting combined with feedback that includes attention to group development issues. The likely reason for the effectiveness of this combined intervention type is that group members set the goals and determine the strategies for improvement themselves. In short, group members and leaders are active as opposed to passive participants in the intervention process. Also, this type of intervention is tailored to the needs of a group at a particular time. It does not assume that one intervention type fits all groups.

Needless to say, research does not suggest that rock climbing, whitewater rafting, blind trust walks, or donkey basketball increases productivity in any way. These kinds of activities are fun for some people and distasteful to others. In any case, there is no evidence that they facilitate changes in group effectiveness or productivity.

Before choosing an intervention to improve group performance, organization members should ask the consultant the following questions:

- What are the underlying assumptions of the intervention? That is, how will the intervention change the dynamics of the group?
- Is the intervention based on solid research evidence?
- Can the consultant provide social science references that support the intervention content?
- Does the intervention work? Do work groups that participate in this type of intervention increase their effectiveness and productivity?

If the consultant cannot answer the first three questions or bases her or his response solely on personal experience, head for the hills. Regarding the fourth question, we can say that although more research is needed, if the intervention includes goal setting, performance feedback, and attention to group development issues, it will work better than other approaches. Until we learn more, it is best to use interventions that contain these three elements.

Avoid Helping Groups Too Much

Many groups get too much help. They may have an array of helpers such as sponsors, coaches, leaders, trainers, and consultants. However, this help is not always helpful. Throughout this chapter, I have outlined the things groups really need to function and to get moving again when they get stuck. I have found no evidence in the literature that increasing the number of expert helpers who meet with the team on a regular basis has any positive effects.

When groups ask for help, they should get the help if it conforms to the guidelines outlined here. Too much help often increases group dependency on experts and reduces the chances that group members will learn to be effective and productive on their own.

I mentioned feedback earlier, but I will mention it again because it is so important: Groups need accurate and frequent feedback about their performance so that they can learn to help themselves. Without feedback, it is very difficult for groups to judge their progress or make corrections to get back on course. Some groups get lots of feedback. Others get almost none. Research tells us that groups that get feedback regularly are more successful.

Make Sure That Each Group Has Enough Autonomy to Do Its Work but Remains Connected With the Rest of the Organization

The mission of every group should be clear to other groups and individuals in the organization. If organization members and units are expected to help each other, they must know what others are doing.

Groups also need sufficient autonomy to do their work. They need to be clear about what decisions they can make on their own and what decisions must be reviewed by others. At the same time, groups must stay in close contact with other organization members and groups. If an isolated group makes a decision without involving others in that decision, the odds of having the decision countermanded or ignored increase significantly. Groups must stay in close contact with others in the organization, because good working relationships with other organization members and groups are important indicators of an effective team.

Conduct Organizational Support Reviews Regularly

Many of the guidelines outlined in this chapter could be read as things that only upper management can accomplish. It is not my intention to imply that. Every member of the organization has a role to play in the success of the groups with which she or he interacts. Each group has a responsibility to solicit the things necessary for its success as well.

Before and during the life of any group, it would be helpful to review these guidelines. Group members or potential members, along with others who interact with the group in some meaningful way, should conduct these reviews to determine the group's level of organizational support and to make changes as needed. Periodic review sessions focused on organizational support, not group performance, will have at least two effects: First, problems with the level of organizational support can be identified and corrected early. Second, group members will be encouraged by the efforts of others to ensure that the group becomes a high performance team.

Organizational support review sessions have not been researched. However, because research has outlined a number of organizational factors that increase the chances of group success, it is only logical that organization members should use such review sessions to ensure that these factors are being addressed.

The following checklist is provided to help people participating in an organizational support review session evaluate the level of organizational support for a particular group. Work group members should complete the checklist anonymously before the meeting. Individual anonymity is crucial to the success of this process. Individuals must feel free to be candid in their responses.

A summary should be prepared before the meeting. At the meeting, participants should discuss the summary and identify areas where organizational support is adequate or superior and areas that need improvement. Action steps should be outlined as well. Although there will be areas where, for legitimate reasons, support cannot be provided at ideal levels, both the work group and the organization it is part of should aim to do the best they can.

The Organizational Support Checklist

Please read the statements below. Circle the number that most accurately describes your response to the statement. Use the following key to respond to each statement.

1 = Disagree strongly

2 = Disagree to some extent

3 = Agree to some extent

4 = Agree strongly

Section I

1. This organization supports innovation.

    1   2   3   4

2. This organization expects to be successful.

    1   2   3   4

3. This organization values superior quality in all work endeavors.

    1   2   3   4

4. Organization members pay attention to detail.

| 1 | 2 | 3 | 4 |

5. This organization values team recommendations.

| 1 | 2 | 3 | 4 |

Section I score: _____

Section II

6. This organization has a clearly defined organizational mission.

| 1 | 2 | 3 | 4 |

7. This organization has clear expectations about the quality of our group's output.

| 1 | 2 | 3 | 4 |

8. This organization has clear expectations for our group's timing and deadlines.

| 1 | 2 | 3 | 4 |

9. Our group's goals are clear to the rest of the organization.

| 1 | 2 | 3 | 4 |

Section II score: _____

Section III

10. The goals and tasks of our group are meaningful.

| 1 | 2 | 3 | 4 |

11. Our group's tasks are interesting to group members.

| 1 | 2 | 3 | 4 |

12. Our group's tasks require group members to work collaboratively.

| 1 | 2 | 3 | 4 |

13. Our group's tasks require continuous learning.

| 1 | 2 | 3 | 4 |

14. Our group has been provided with members with appropriate technical skills.

| 1 | 2 | 3 | 4 |

(Continued)

(Continued)

Section III score: _____

Section IV

15. Our group has access to the technical resources necessary to accomplish its tasks.

    1   2   3   4

16. Our group has access to the human resources necessary to accomplish its tasks.

    1   2   3   4

17. Our group has a defined work area.

    1   2   3   4

18. Our group has sufficient autonomy to do its work.

    1   2   3   4

19. Our group is in close communication with appropriate organization members and groups.

    1   2   3   4

Section IV score: _____

Section V

20. Our group receives regular feedback about its performance and progress.

    1   2   3   4

21. Our group receives positive recognition for group achievements.

    1   2   3   4

22. Rewards and recognition are based on group achievements.

    1   2   3   4

Section V score: _____

Section VI

23. Our group has been provided with members with skills in the area of group participation.

    1   2   3   4

24. Our group has been provided with a leader with skills in the areas of group management and group participation.

      1   2   3   4

25. Our group has been provided with all technical training necessary for group success.

      1   2   3   4

26. Our group has been provided with appropriate team training.

      1   2   3   4

27. Our group leader has been provided with appropriate leadership training.

      1   2   3   4

28. Our group has been provided with the help of consultants when it has been deemed necessary for group success.

      1   2   3   4

Section VI score: _____

Section VII

If group training has been provided to your group, please answer the following questions:

29. I learned what I needed to know to work successfully with this group.

      1   2   3   4

30. I felt that the trainer was competent.

      1   2   3   4

If group consultation has been provided to your group, please answer the following questions:

31. The consultation helped the group members to work more effectively together.

      1   2   3   4

32. I felt that the consultant was competent.

      1   2   3   4

Section VII score: _____

(Continued)

(Continued)

Maximum score: 128
Minimum score: 32
My score: _____

What is the overall level of organizational support?

Total Score	Organization's Grade
115+	A
103–114	B
89–102	C

What are the section scores?

Section I: Organizational Culture

Total Score	Organization's Grade
18+	A
16–17	B
14–15	C

Section II: Mission Clarity

Total Score	Organization's Grade
14+	A
12–13	B
10–11	C

Section III: Task and Technology

Total Score	Organization's Grade
18+	A
16–17	B
14–15	C

Section IV: Autonomy and Access

Total Score	Organization's Grade
14+	A
12–13	B
10–11	C

Section V: Feedback and Recognition

Total Score	Organization's Grade
11+	A
9–10	B
7–8	C

Section VI: Training and Development

Total Score	Organization's Grade
22+	A
19–21	B
16–18	C

Section VII: Training Quality

Total Score	Organization's Grade
14+	A
12–13	B
10–11	C

THREE

FROM GROUPS TO TEAMS

The Stages of Group Development

———◆———

Groups develop across time very much as people do. People experience childhood, adolescence, young adulthood, adulthood, and old age. Childhood is associated with dependency. Adolescence usually contains periods of conflict. Young adulthood requires a lot of time spent developing trusting relationships and preparing for a career. In adulthood people spend a significant amount of time working, and in old age people typically reduce their focus on work.

Research has found that groups also experience periods of dependency, conflict, trust and structuring, work, and disengagement. Group development and human development have much in common.

The concept of group development is well documented in the social science literature. In view of the general consensus that groups develop and change across time, extensive reviews of the literature have been conducted to consolidate previous research and to propose a unified model of group development. These reviews have produced similar results. What follows is a brief description of the integrated model of group development that I use in my own work. This model was initially based on previous research. Since then, a number of studies have been conducted to determine whether these stages actually occur in work groups. These studies have confirmed that the stages of development outlined in the model do occur in groups in the real world.

Stage 1: Dependency and Inclusion

The first stage of group development is characterized by members' dependency on the designated leader, concerns about safety, and concerns about feeling included in the group. This first stage of group development may manifest itself as members' compliance with plans proposed by the group leader or by a powerful member. Group members often engage in what has been called pseudo work, or flight, such as exchanging stories about customers or their families that are irrelevant to the task at hand. Members may also wait for the group leader to make decisions. In fact, members often urge the leader to take charge and tell them what to do. Members seem more concerned about being accepted by others than about the task at hand. They are unlikely to express different points of view as a result.

Identifying a Stage 1 Group

- Members are concerned about personal safety in the group
- Members are concerned about acceptance and inclusion by others in the group
- Members fear rejection
- Members communicate in tentative and very polite ways
- Members express a need for dependable and directive leadership
- Members see the leader as benevolent and competent
- Members expect and encourage the leader to provide them with direction and personal safety
- Members very rarely challenge the leader
- The group's goals are not clear to its members, but members don't try to clarify them
- Members rarely express disagreement with the group's initial goals
- The group assumes that there is consensus about its goals
- Role assignments tend to be based on external status, first impressions, and initial self-presentation rather than on matching member competencies with goals and task requirements
- Member compliance is high
- Communication tends to go through the leader
- Participation is generally limited to a few vocal members

- Conflict is minimal
- Conformity is high
- A lack of group structure and organization is evident
- Member deviation from emerging norms is rare
- Cohesion and commitment to the group are based on identification with the leader
- Subgroups and coalitions are rare

Box 3.1   Silence of the Lambs

You know you're in a Stage 1 group when the leader asks a question and no one responds. The leader's words seem to vanish into the Bermuda Triangle.

Stage 2: Counterdependency and Fighting

At Stage 2, the group seeks to free itself from its dependence on the leader, and members fight about group goals and procedures. Task conflict is an inevitable part of this process. The group's task at this stage is to develop a unified set of goals, values, and operational procedures, and this task usually generates conflict. Task conflict also is necessary for the establishment of trust and a climate in which members feel free to disagree with each other.

Some groups become mired in interpersonal conflicts and remain stuck at this developmental stage. Other groups are overwhelmed by the stress of this phase and revert to leader dependence in an attempt to avoid further conflict. Research tells us that task conflict is essential if teams are to become effective and productive. However, interpersonal conflict can stop a work group in its tracks. When disagreements become personal, trust is lost and members do not feel safe in the group. Stay focused on work tasks and avoid conflicts that are based on personality or incompatibility.

Box 3.2   Toxic Waste

You know you're in a Stage 2 group when the thought of going to a team meeting makes you feel ill.

Neither remaining stuck in Stage 2 nor regressing to Stage 1 has positive effects for the group or for the quality of work generated by the group. Only through resolution of task conflicts and the development of a unified view of the group's purpose and procedures can true collaboration be achieved.

Identifying a Stage 2 Group

- Conflicts about values emerge
- Disagreements about goals and tasks emerge
- Increased feelings of safety allow dissent to occur
- Dissatisfaction with roles may surface
- Goal clarification begins
- Role clarification begins
- Members challenge the leader and each other
- Subgroups and coalitions form
- Group intolerance of subgroups, cliques, and coalitions is evident
- Member participation increases
- Conformity decreases
- Deviation from emerging group norms begins to occur
- Attempts at conflict management begin
- If efforts to resolve conflicts are successful, consensus about group goals and culture increases near the end of this stage
- Conflict resolution, if successful, increases trust and cohesion

Stage 3: Trust and Structure

If a group manages to work through the inevitable conflicts of Stage 2, member trust, commitment to the group, and willingness to cooperate increase. Communication becomes more open and task oriented. Professional territoriality decreases as members focus more on the task and less on issues of status, power, or influence. This third stage of group development is characterized by more mature negotiations about roles, organization, and procedures. It is also a time in which members work to solidify positive working relationships with each other.

Identifying a Stage 3 Group

- Goal clarity and consensus increase
- Roles and tasks are adjusted to increase the likelihood of goal achievement

- The leader's role becomes less directive and more consultative
- The communication structure becomes more flexible
- The content of communication becomes more task oriented
- Pressures to conform increase again
- Helpful deviation is tolerated
- Coalitions and subgroups continue to emerge
- Tolerance of subgroups, cliques, and coalitions increases
- Cohesion and trust increase
- Member satisfaction increases
- Cooperation is more evident
- Individual commitment to group goals and tasks is high
- Greater division of labor occurs
- Conflict continues to occur, but it is managed more effectively
- The group works to clarify and build a group structure that will facilitate goal achievement

Stage 4: Work

As its name implies, the fourth stage of group development is a time of intense team productivity and effectiveness. At this stage, the group becomes a high performance team. Having resolved many of the issues of the previous stages, the team can focus more of its energies on goal achievement and task accomplishment. Although some work occurs at every developmental stage, the quality and quantity of work increase significantly during Stage 4.

Whenever I teach or give a talk or presentation, I describe Stage 4 and ask audience members to raise their hand if they have ever been a member of a Stage 4 group. About one in four people raise their hand. That, coupled with the fact that only a small percentage of the groups in my database are Stage 4 groups, as described in Chapter 2, leads me to believe that many readers of this book have never been a member of a Stage 4 group. So read this next section carefully. Working in a Stage 4 group is a wonderful experience.

Identifying a Stage 4 Group

- Members are clear about the team's goals
- Members agree with the team's goals
- Tasks require a team rather than individual effort

- Members are clear about their roles
- Members accept their roles and status in the team
- Role assignments match member abilities
- Delegation or "unleadership" is the prevailing leadership style
- The team's communication structure matches the demands of the task
- The team has an open communication structure in which all members participate and are heard
- The team has an appropriate ratio of task communications to supportive communications
- The team gets, gives, and uses feedback about its effectiveness and productivity
- The team spends time defining problems it must solve or decisions it must make
- The team spends time planning how it will solve problems and make decisions
- The team spends enough time discussing its problems and decisions
- The team uses participatory decision-making methods
- The team implements and evaluates its decisions and solutions to problems
- Voluntary conformity is high
- Task-related deviance is tolerated
- Team norms encourage high performance and quality
- The team expects to be successful
- The team encourages innovation
- Team members pay attention to the details of their work
- The team accepts coalition and subgroup formation
- Subgroups are integrated into the team as a whole
- Subgroups work on important tasks
- Tasks contain variety and challenge
- Each subgroup works on a total product or project
- The team contains the smallest number of members necessary to accomplish its goals
- Subgroups are recognized and rewarded by the team
- The team is highly cohesive
- Interpersonal attraction between members is high
- Members are cooperative
- Periods of conflict are frequent but brief
- The team has effective conflict management strategies

Box 3.3   Pride in the Work

You know you're in a Stage 4 group when you can't wait to get to the team meeting because it's exhilarating, fun, and important and makes you feel like a grown-up.

Box 3.4   The Stages of Group Development

1. Dependency and Inclusion
2. Counterdependency and Fighting
3. Trust and Structure
4. Work and Productivity

Group development does not always proceed in a positive direction. Groups can get stuck at a particular stage for an extended period of time, resulting in long-term ineffectiveness and low productivity. Also, groups may fluctuate widely based on the circumstances and forces affecting them at a given moment. Changes in membership, external demands, and changes in leadership can all affect the work of a group. Turnover rates, reassignments, and new upper-level managers often produce regression and necessitate the rebuilding of group structures and culture.

Not all work groups, of any type, achieve adequate levels of effectiveness and productivity. In fact, some studies estimate that between 80% and 90% of all groups have difficulties with performance. Although achieving an effective performance level is difficult for any group, it is even more problematic for groups with diverse members. Groups composed of members from different professions, for example, have additional obstacles to productivity. These include the lack of an organizing framework, issues of professional territoriality, and miscommunication. The road to productivity is fraught with difficulties.

Surviving Group Development

There are a few things people can do, and a few attitudes people can take on, that make the process of group development easier. Like human beings, groups have some rocky times on the road to maturity. Here are a few suggestions to help group members survive, and even enjoy, the process of group development.

Learn About Group Development

It helps to know what's in store for you as you move through the various stages of individual human development. For example, when social scientists determined that adults experience developmental stages, some of which are not so pleasant, we all breathed a sigh of relief. Once we started talking about adolescent insecurities, midlife crises, menopause, and the like, many people stopped feeling alone and out of control. Instead of feeling scared or depressed, people felt normal. Other people were experiencing the same things, and that made individuals feel better. Knowledge of developmental stages also makes an individual's experiences at a particular age seem more manageable. Finally, this knowledge usually leads to better, happier individual development.

The same is true of group development. When group members know that all groups go through predictable stages of development, they can relax and enjoy the ride. When groups don't know about group development, their members might think that their fellow group members are strange or that their particular group is extremely dysfunctional or unusual. Clearly, people with knowledge of group behavior make better group members and leaders. Such knowledgeable people are less likely to misinterpret what they see and more likely to be constructive in what they say and do.

Be Patient

Although human development and group development have a lot in common, group development doesn't take as long. However, it does take some time. My colleagues and I have been monitoring the progress of hundreds of groups over the years, and we have yet to see a high performance team that had been meeting for less than six months. For the first two or three months, groups are dealing with the issues characteristic of Stages 1 and 2. Groups generally enter Stage 3 in the fourth or fifth month, and Stage 4, or high performance, typically begins during the sixth or seventh month. Of course, this is assuming that a group does not run into any snags.

Most people in upper management and in groups don't understand that groups develop over time. They want groups to function at high levels from the beginning. That simply doesn't happen. It takes time to figure out what the goals really mean. It takes time to figure out how to accomplish those goals and who should do what. It takes time to resolve problems and disagreements that come up. It's important to be patient.

Unfortunately, some groups, like some people, never mature. They stay stuck in dependency or conflict for as long as the group exists. Other groups manage to become high performance teams only to regress to earlier stages later on. This is usually due to some internal crisis or a change in the level of organizational support.

Fortunately, no group has to stay stuck or regressed. If members are willing to work to turn things around, it can be done.

Expect Things to Be Murky at the Beginning of a Group

Things are never clear at the beginning of a group. Often, after an early meeting, you'll hear people asking each other questions about what went on during the meeting. Of course, no one asked those questions during the meeting. This is normal, and as time goes on people will begin to feel free to ask for clarification during group meetings. A person who expects a new group to have a perfectly organized meeting with clear outcomes will be disappointed. This person might even get angry, and that will do no one any good.

Expect Conflict and Treat It as a Positive Sign of Progress

Most of us avoid conflict as much as we can. The problem in groups, as in life, is that conflict is inevitable. Each group has to define its goals, clarify how it will function, and determine the various roles that members will play. Group members should expect disagreements about the content of the group's goal and how to solve specific problems related to that goal. Task conflict is a necessary part of this process because, from divergent points of view, a more unified direction must be agreed upon if group members are to work together in a productive way.

On a more psychological level, task conflict is necessary for the establishment of a safe environment. Although at first glance this may seem paradoxical, task conflict promotes the development of trust. We all know from our own experience that it is easier to develop trust in another person or in a group if we believe that we can disagree and we won't be abandoned or hurt because we have a different perspective. It is difficult to trust those who deny us the right to hold different views. To engage in a task conflict with others and to work it out is an exhilarating experience. It provides energy, a shared experience, and a sense of safety and authenticity and allows deeper trust levels and collaboration.

From the task perspective, if people are not free to express their points of view, the group's product is likely to be inferior. If everyone just goes along with the first idea that's expressed, the outcome is unlikely to be of high quality. Task conflict is a normal, natural, and necessary part of group life. Keeping that in mind will make things much easier.

Help the Group Limit Conflicts to Those About Tasks, Roles, Structures, and the Like; Don't Get Involved in Personal Feuds or Personality Conflicts

Although conflict may be normal and necessary, some kinds of conflict can be very detrimental to group development. Personal feuds and personality conflicts that erupt in groups can cause group progress to cease, sometimes permanently. The problem with personal conflicts is that they usually can't be resolved. If one person doesn't like another's personality, the rest of the group can't really do anything about it. However, what appear to be personality conflicts are often really the results of other factors in the group that can be addressed, such as goal confusion and role assignments. The group can deal with these things more successfully. In general, it's good to disagree about goals, tasks, roles, and so on. It's not good for group members to personalize these things and see other members as bad or incompetent because they have a different opinion or a different way of doing things.

Compromise on Issues When Possible and Help Others Resolve Differences

In the course of my research, I have attended or listened to tapes of many group meetings. Sometimes members are disagreeing and no one is willing to compromise. Although I would not advocate compromise on an issue that is really important to group success or that has ethical consequences, compromise is essential to group productivity.

One example of unwillingness to compromise stands out in my mind. A certain group was working on a very important new product for the company. The company had had a recent layoff, and more layoffs were anticipated. The group was over budget and had missed several deadlines. During my observation, a conflict unrelated to the goal of the group kept emerging. Members had taken sides on this issue, and neither side was willing to give in. This story has a happy ending. I worked with the group and helped them to see that this conflict about who was right and who was wrong would ultimately result in group failure. Most stories like this don't have happy endings.

Don't Sit on the Sidelines; Take Responsibility for What Is Going On, Even If It Doesn't Involve You Directly

Every group member is responsible for the group's outcomes. Group members shouldn't wait for other members or the leader to solve a problem or save the day. Members should make suggestions and share their ideas, concerns, and reservations. Of course, it helps if they can do this in a diplomatic way.

Be Supportive of Other Members and the Leader

Some of the research that my colleagues and I have conducted over the years has required us to put each verbal statement made by group members into one of a number of categories. Here are examples of supportive statements:

"Thanks for that suggestion, Joe."

"I appreciate your saying that, Mary."

"I agree with you, Abe."

In groups that are doing well, out of every 100 statements made by group members, between 15 and 20 are supportive statements. That sounds like a lot, but we see this over and over again. There's nothing like a little support to encourage people to work to capacity.

Complete Your Tasks in a Timely Fashion

Groups are not groups just during meetings. Group members work together and separately outside the group to complete work related to the group's goals. Nothing slows down group progress more than failure to accomplish those tasks in a timely fashion. Trust is built between members not by words but by actions. If group members can trust each other to do what they say, things will go very smoothly.

Don't Be Upset When Subgroups or Coalitions Emerge

Sometimes subgroups are formed when they are needed to get a group's work done. At other times, group members will form a coalition with others to emphasize a point they're trying to make. These are natural and good things, but the existence of subgroups and coalitions upsets some people. These people may feel left out or believe that the presence of smaller units within the group will interfere with the group's success. Some group members call these subgroups "cliques," which has negative connotations. However, the presence of subgroups generally is not negative. It is a sign that the group is getting organized and will be able to get its work done during the inevitable crunch time. Coalitions can help the group to see another point of view, which often turns out to be the right one.

Of course, subgroups and coalitions can have negative effects sometimes. When coalitions are unwilling to compromise, for example, things can go awry. When subgroups take action without checking with or informing the whole group, the results can be negative. Most of the time, however, the appearance of subgroups and coalitions is a healthy sign of group progress.

Encourage Your Group to Regularly Assess How It Is Functioning

People at work these days are very busy. They want the meeting to end quickly so that they can deal with the piles of work on their desks. The last thing people want to do is take five minutes out of the meeting to discuss how they are working together. The very last thing they want to do is spend an entire meeting every two months or so discussing how the group is functioning. That seems like a big waste of time. I encourage groups to do it anyway. In the long run, it will save time and aggravation. More on how to assess group progress regularly can be found in Chapter 10.

Show Up

I once worked with a group in which the membership changed almost weekly. There were 20 people in this planning group. Each week about 10 people showed up, and those 10 were different almost every time. There is nothing like unstable membership to slow group development or to stop it altogether. Each meeting becomes a repeat of the last, and the focus becomes catching people up on what happened at the last meeting.

In later chapters, I will offer more suggestions to members and leaders about what they can do to help their groups be successful.

FOUR

HOW DO HIGH PERFORMANCE TEAMS FUNCTION?

S ome people I've come across think that all this focus on team development is a waste of time. They ask whether any of this effort makes a difference to the bottom line. They are usually very surprised when I tell them that it does. For example, work teams functioning at the higher stages of group development finish projects faster, produce products of higher quality, and generate more revenue than groups functioning at the lower stages of group development. Students taught by faculty teams functioning at the higher stages of group development score higher on standardized tests. Intensive care staff teams functioning at higher stages of group development save more lives. Paying attention to group development is the key to successful outcomes.

People are right to be skeptical about lots of the things currently being done to increase team effectiveness and productivity. Many of those things actually are a waste of time. However, there are things that high performance teams do that make a very real difference to the bottom line.

The Characteristics of High Performance Teams

Research studies on the relationship between internal team processes and productivity have identified a number of characteristics of high performance teams that are associated with productivity:

- Members are clear about and agree with the team's goals
- Tasks are appropriate to team rather than individual solutions

- Members are clear about and accept their roles
- Role assignments match members' abilities
- The leadership style matches the team's development level
- An open communication structure allows all members to participate
- The team gets, gives, and uses feedback about its effectiveness and productivity
- The team spends time defining and discussing problems it must solve or decisions it must make
- Members also spend time planning how they will solve problems and make decisions
- The team uses effective decision-making strategies
- The team implements and evaluates its solutions and decisions
- Task-related deviance is tolerated
- Team norms encourage high performance, quality, success, and innovation
- Subgroups are integrated into the team as a whole
- The team contains the smallest number of members necessary to accomplish its goals
- Team members have sufficient time together to develop a mature working unit and to accomplish the team's goals
- The team is highly cohesive and cooperative
- Periods of conflict are frequent but brief, and the group has effective conflict management strategies

Box 4.1   Education Matters
Faculty groups at higher stages of group development have a significantly higher percentage of students who pass statewide proficiency tests than faculty groups at lower stages of group development.

10 Keys to Productivity

The previous list of the characteristics of high performance teams suggests that there are 10 key areas that members should pay attention to in order to ensure the productivity of their group:

1. Goals

2. Roles

3. Interdependence

4. Leadership

5. Communication and feedback

6. Discussion, decision making, and planning

7. Implementation and evaluation

8. Norms and individual differences

9. Structure

10. Cooperation and conflict management

Each of these areas is discussed next.

Goals

The most important characteristic of a high performance team is that its members are clear about the team's goals. Although this seems obvious, I have seen too many groups in which this was not the case. Even if all the group members seem to know what the goals are, they often have different ideas about what accomplishing them entails. Even if people are saying the same words, those words may mean different things to different people. For example, I remember a group that was established to develop a strategic plan for a division of a large organization. Each member knew what the goal was, but there were different opinions about what developing a strategic plan actually meant. For some, developing a strategic plan meant engaging in a lengthy process of collecting data from organization members, competitors, and customers; reading literature about the industry; and making predictions about future trends in the industry. Once that information was collected and analyzed, the group would devise a decision-making process that involved members and customers. Finally, the group would formulate a strategic plan.

Others in the group had a very different view of what it meant to develop a strategic plan. For them, it meant holding two or three committee meetings, discussing ideas about what the division should do over the next five years, and writing up the ideas that the majority of committee members agreed with.

This example underscores the necessity of thoroughly discussing group goals and what those goals mean to different group members. Until everyone is clear about the goals, it makes no sense to try to accomplish them.

Even after everyone is clear about the group's goals, it does not necessarily follow that everyone agrees with the goals. However, one of the characteristics of high performance teams is that members agree with the team's goals. This means that they think the goals are important, reasonable, and attainable and will benefit the team as well as the organization.

I do not mean to imply that people must think that every group goal is the best thing since sliced bread or the most exciting assignment they have ever been given. Some goals (e.g., cutting the budget, reducing overhead, changing the shipping schedule) are not very exciting but may be important to the team and the organization. The point is that members need to see the relevance of the goals if the team is to be successful.

Roles

Once group members have clarified the group's goals and agree on them, they can begin to organize themselves to accomplish those goals. This usually includes deciding what needs to be done and who should do what.

Using the previous example as a case in point, let's imagine that group members have agreed that the tasks involved in developing a strategic plan are as follows:

1. Collecting data from organization members

2. Collecting data from competitors

3. Collecting data from customers

4. Reading literature about the current state of the industry

5. Reading literature about future trends in the industry

6. Analyzing the data

7. Developing a decision-making process involving organization members and customers

After lengthy discussions about how each of these tasks might be accomplished, decisions about which member or members should work on each task must be made. Often, people volunteer to take on certain tasks, or the group leader assigns them to tasks. Neither of these options is inherently good or bad. Three things are crucial, however. First, each member must be clear about the role she or he is being asked to play. That is, the expectations must be clear, and the process for accomplishing the assigned task must be clear as well. Second, each member must have the ability and skills necessary to accomplish the assigned or chosen task. Third, each member must agree with and accept the assigned role.

Again, these requirements for assigning roles seem obvious. In reality, however, it is a rare group that meets these requirements. There are many reasons for this failure to ensure that members are clear about their roles, have the abilities necessary to accomplish them, and are willing to take on the roles they have been assigned. Here are just a few examples of how good people set themselves up to fail:

- Mary volunteers to collect data from organization members. She is new to the company and doesn't know too many people yet. She has worked for three competitors and would be more valuable in helping to collect information about competitors. Because she volunteered, however, no one is willing to raise any of these issues.
- Joe volunteers to review the literature about current and future trends in the industry. He is not computer literate, however, and much of the information will have to be gathered through online databases and the Internet. Again, because he volunteered, no one raised these concerns.
- The group's leader, John, volunteers to analyze the data as it comes in. Sarah is a statistician and would be perfect for this job, but because John is the leader, no one questions his right to assign himself this task.

Interdependence

In successful teams, tasks require team members to work together as a unit and in subgroups. In the case of a team developing a strategic plan, because the amount of work involved to reach that goal is well beyond the ability of a single individual, members need to work together as a unit and in subgroups.

In addition, the goal requires interdependence, because a strategic plan developed by one person is not likely to reflect the division accurately. A successful strategic plan is one that works. The team working to create such a plan needs to incorporate many viewpoints, accurately interpret and sift through those differing views, and develop a plan that is acceptable to others and will lead the division in a positive direction. This is one of the best reasons for using a group rather than an individual to accomplish certain goals. A well-functioning team will beat an individual in accomplishing this type of goal any day.

Leadership

In productive teams, the leader's style changes when necessary to meet emerging group needs. Members' perceptions of the role of the leader also change at different stages of group development. At Stage 1, group members perceive the leader as benevolent and powerful. She or he is perceived as the source of members' safety and reward. At this stage, members expect the leader to be directive. At Stage 2, however, members begin to challenge the leader's authority and control. In order for the group to mature, such challenges are necessary. The role of the leader must be redefined if the group is to move into the more mature stages of development. Stage 2 leaders should still remain directive and gradually begin to involve members in discussing options and exploring issues. By the time a group has reached the third stage of development, group members have assumed many of the roles that initially were the domain of the leader. Finally, at Stage 4, effective leaders act like expert members. Most of the leader's functions have been distributed among team members.

In high performance teams, members assume many of the functions that leaders performed at earlier stages. For this to occur, the leader's role must become less directive and more consultative. The leader can help to redistribute power among members by altering her or his leadership style to match the needs of the group. This requires that the leader know what the needs of the group are at any given time and how to behave to facilitate movement. If a leader maintains one style of leadership throughout the life of a group, she or he will not meet group needs and will not facilitate the development of a high performance team. More information about effective leadership can be found in Chapter 6.

Communication and Feedback

High performance teams have an open communication structure that allows all members to participate. Individuals are listened to regardless of their age, title, sex, race, ethnicity, profession, or other status characteristics. This increases productivity because all ideas and suggestions get heard.

High performance teams get regular feedback about their effectiveness and productivity. When members are asked to assess the team's effectiveness and productivity, they are able to answer accurately. This means that members seek feedback about how the team is performing from each other and from external sources.

Members of high performance teams give each other constructive feedback about individual performance and contributions. Constructive feedback promotes improvement and individual development. That is, the feedback is intended to be helpful to the team by improving member efforts to accomplish goals. It is also intended to be helpful to the individual by providing information that she or he can use to become a more effective team member. If feedback does not meet both of these criteria, it should not be given.

Finally, high performance teams use feedback about team processes and productivity to make improvements in how they are functioning. You would be surprised at the number of groups I have encountered whose members receive feedback about group performance but do not use that feedback to implement constructive changes. In most cases, this is due to a simple flaw in the group's internal processes. Groups that do not use feedback constructively usually do not have a mechanism in place to evaluate the validity of the feedback and to make decisions about what changes should be made based on that feedback. An example of such a mechanism might be one where internal and external feedback are sought on a regular basis and where the feedback is discussed and evaluated at the beginning of the next meeting. If the feedback is judged to be valid and helpful, members discuss ways to improve team performance, decide what changes to make, and implement those changes.

This may seem like an elaborate process, but in reality it usually takes 10 minutes or less. The trick is to collect the feedback from members at the end of one session and discuss it at the beginning of the next. Feedback from external sources should be collected between meetings.

Discussion, Decision Making, and Planning

Members of high performance teams spend time planning how they will solve problems and make decisions. That is, they determine how decisions will be made before they attempt to make decisions. They may decide that majority vote, a two-thirds majority vote, consensus, or another decision-making strategy will be used. The key is that these determinations are made in advance and that the team's decision-making strategy is effective and meets with member approval.

Also, members of high performance teams spend time defining and discussing problems they must solve. That is, in advance of a final decision, sufficient discussion has occurred so that everyone is clear about the issues involved and the alternative ways of dealing with those issues. If insufficient time is spent in discussion before a decision is made, the resulting decision may be inadequate or in error.

Implementation and Evaluation

High performance teams implement the solutions and decisions made by members. That is, members and the leader follow up on those decisions and hold each other accountable for acting on those decisions. Teams that are successful also develop methods to evaluate team solutions and decisions. Decisions may turn out to be in error or inadequate, but in effective teams those errors or inadequacies are caught and corrected quickly.

Norms and Individual Differences

Successful teams establish norms that encourage high performance, quality, and success. Such teams also have norms that encourage members to be creative and innovative. It would be difficult, if not impossible, for a team to be successful if its members were not expected to perform at high levels.

Another interesting characteristic of effective teams is that members who behave differently are accepted as long as their behavior is perceived as helpful to task accomplishment. For example, if a member does not talk as much as other members expect, that member will be accepted as long as the contributions she or he does make are considered helpful. A member who seems loud or a bit aggressive also will be accepted if her or his task-related performance is perceived as useful. In short, successful teams contain members who tolerate, or even enjoy, each other's idiosyncrasies in order to get the job done.

Structure

Three factors are important to the structure of successful teams. First, successful teams contain the smallest number of members necessary to accomplish goals and tasks. In a recent study, I investigated 329 work groups to determine whether the size of these groups influenced productivity. The results were clear. Groups containing three to six members are significantly more productive than larger groups. Second, the hallmark of a mature team is that members are able to form subgroups to get work done. Third, subgroups are not perceived as threatening by members who are not part of these groups. Instead, subgroups are accepted and valued for their contribution to the team. Subgroups are not seen as renegade or revolutionary groups. Rather, subgroups are integrated into the team as a whole. In short, productive teams are organized. In addition, these teams have sufficient time together, overall and at each meeting, to develop and maintain high performance and to accomplish goals.

This last point is worth emphasizing. Most groups need eight or nine months together to be successful. I base this time estimate on the research I described earlier that suggests it takes at least six months for a group to mature fully. Requirements for the length of individual meetings vary with the complexity of the group's goals. Many meetings are simply too short, however. In my experience, the most tragic examples of this occur in schools. Elementary, middle, and high school teachers are expected to deal with complex matters. Their responsibilities include coordinating the curriculum, developing interdisciplinary lesson plans, and monitoring the behavior and progress of students taught by a number of faculty members, just to name a few. In general, the faculty of a school meets as a whole group once a month or less and for about an hour. Faculty subgroups (e.g., the seventh-grade teachers) meet more frequently. These subgroups usually meet for 45 minutes once a week. Of course, 45 minutes is actually 30 or 35 minutes, because teachers need time to dismiss their students and to settle into the meeting. Teachers also have to leave before the end of the allotted time in order to get to their next class on time, making it difficult for them to have meaningful and thorough discussion, planning, and decision making.

Each group will have to judge for itself how much time it will need to accomplish its goals and how long each meeting should be. It's important that a group not shortchange itself or set itself up for failure by not allowing enough time or by using time inefficiently. Individual members and subgroups can do many tasks between meetings.

Cooperation and Conflict Management

A large body of research confirms that a high performance team is highly cohesive and contains cooperative members. Of course, cooperation alone is insufficient to achieve success. The other factors outlined in this chapter must be in evidence as well. For example, in some groups, members cooperate to avoid work. In others, members cooperate to do the minimum amount of work. Clearly, cooperation is not enough, but without it success is very unlikely.

That members cooperate does not mean that conflict never occurs. In fact, research tells us that productive teams have frequent but brief periods of task conflict. Task conflicts are brief because high performance teams have effective conflict management strategies.

Productive teams operate differently than unproductive groups. Productivity is not an accident or the result of one or two people. The way a group functions, from the beginning, does make a difference in its productivity. Studies have found that high performance teams actually produce more than other work groups. They are also rated as more productive by their managers, and their members rate their team as more productive. These studies have been conducted in the financial industry, the hotel industry, the manufacturing sector, the service sector, the healthcare industry, and educational institutions.

It's not a waste of time to pay attention to how your group is functioning. Based on what we now know, it's clear that time spent on improving the functioning of your group is time well spent. It might be helpful for your group to review the characteristics of high performance teams and determine what your group is doing well and what needs improvement. Use the Team Performance Checklist in this chapter to assess your group's current level of effectiveness. Collate members' responses to questions and determine the group's average score. If that score is 85 or above, you can legitimately call yourselves members of a high performance team. Regardless of the score, there will be areas that need improvement. Plan ways to make the necessary improvements.

Team Performance Checklist

Please read the statements below. Circle the number that most accurately describes your response to the statement. Use the following key to respond to each statement:

1 = Disagree strongly

2 = Disagree to some extent

3 = Agree to some extent

4 = Agree strongly

1. Members are clear about group goals.

   1   2   3   4

2. Members agree with group goals.

   1   2   3   4

3. Group tasks require members to work together.

   1   2   3   4

4. Members are clear about their roles.

   1   2   3   4

5. Members accept their roles.

   1   2   3   4

6. Members' assignments match their abilities.

   1   2   3   4

7. The group leader's style changes when necessary to meet emerging group needs.

   1   2   3   4

8. The group has an open communication structure that allows all members to participate.

   1   2   3   4

9. The group gets regular feedback about its productivity.

   1   2   3   4

10. Members give each other constructive feedback.

    1   2   3   4

11. The group uses feedback about its effectiveness to make improvements in how it is functioning.

     1   2   3   4

12. The group spends time defining and discussing problems it must solve.

     1   2   3   4

13. Members spend time planning how they will solve problems and make decisions.

     1   2   3   4

14. The group uses effective decision-making strategies.

     1   2   3   4

15. The group implements its solutions and decisions.

     1   2   3   4

16. The group develops methods to evaluate its solutions and decisions.

     1   2   3   4

17. The group accepts members who behave differently as long as their behavior is perceived as helpful to task accomplishment.

     1   2   3   4

18. Group norms encourage high performance, quality, and success.

     1   2   3   4

19. Group norms encourage innovative solutions.

     1   2   3   4

20. Subgroups are accepted and integrated into the group as a whole.

     1   2   3   4

21. The group contains the smallest number of members necessary to accomplish its goals.

     1   2   3   4

(Continued)

(Continued)

22. The group has been given sufficient time to develop a mature working unit and to accomplish its goals.

| 1 | 2 | 3 | 4 |

23. The group is highly cohesive and cooperative.

| 1 | 2 | 3 | 4 |

24. Periods of conflict are frequent but brief.

| 1 | 2 | 3 | 4 |

25. The group uses effective conflict management strategies.

| 1 | 2 | 3 | 4 |

Minimum score: 25

Maximum score: 100

Your group's average score: _____

What is your group's stage of development?

Total Score	Group's Stage
85+	4
70–84	3
<70	1* or 2**

*The group is in Stage 1 if members are tentative, polite, and somewhat passive.

**The group is in Stage 2 if members are disagreeing with each other or the leader.

⊰ FIVE ⊱

EFFECTIVE TEAM MEMBERS

————•❖•————

S
o much has been written about leaders that it would take at least one large library to house all the books, journals, magazines, and other materials that focus on leadership. Materials that focus on membership still fit neatly in a corner on my desk. Leadership training and coaching leaders abound. In all likelihood, you have attended leadership training at some point in your career. But have you been to membership training? Sadly, I think your answer would be no. Have you ever seen a brochure or ad in a professional journal that describes a membership training workshop? I haven't, and advertisements for training cross my desk almost every day. Besides, who wants to go to membership training? It would be like volunteering for a remedial class in high school. Winners go to leadership training. Only losers need to learn how to be effective members.

Of course, nothing could be further from the truth. Unless all members work to ensure group success, it won't happen. Leaders and members all have to put their oars in the water and row in the same direction to reach the group's goals. No one gets to be a bystander in the process of group development.

Actually, I'm getting tired of writing about the lack of work group membership training. The first edition of *Creating Effective Teams* was published in 1999. It's now 2014, and nothing much has changed in the membership training department. Membership training hasn't caught on. It's not fair to ask people to participate in a group at work without helping them acquire the skills they need to be effective members. For my part, I no longer offer leadership training. Instead, I train work groups in effective membership and effective leadership. Members and leaders of real work groups learn together and learn each other's roles. This approach is much more effective because the attitudes and skills participants acquire can be put to use at the group's next meeting. Also, members and the leader can help each other become more effective by supporting each other and offering advice.

This chapter outlines what research tells us about the behaviors and attitudes of effective team members. These are presented in the form of guidelines. None of these characteristics requires any special personality type, but they all require goodwill and some degree of effort. As you read the chapter, think about a group you are working with at the moment. Ask yourself the following questions:

- Do I follow these guidelines?
- Can I think of times when I exhibited these behaviors and attitudes?
- Can I think of times when I should have exhibited these behaviors but, for some reason, did not?
- In what areas do I need to improve?
- What do I plan to do to improve in those areas?

If you're going to be an effective team member, you'll need to take a closer look at your own behaviors and attitudes and at the way you interact with the group. Here are some guidelines to help you evaluate your performance as a group member.

Don't Blame Others for Group Problems

One of the more difficult problems I encounter in working with groups is a general feeling of helplessness. Somehow, members of groups are convinced that they can't make a difference. I hear lots of statements like the following:

"Unless the leader is replaced, there's nothing the rest of us can do."

"These people are crazy. I don't even want to come to meetings."

"Team meetings are like swimming with sharks. I just keep my head down."

"Our meetings are a waste of time. I wish the leader were stronger."

"I'm not even sure what we're supposed to be doing, but I'm afraid to ask."

"The same people talk in circles. I just keep quiet and hope the meeting will end soon."

"There's nothing we can do. Upper management has to get into the act before things will change."

I encounter these feelings of helplessness very often among people in the workplace. Of course, I realize that things can be pretty chaotic in organizations due to downsizing, mergers, new initiatives, recessions, and the like, but I am not convinced that those are the only reasons for the passivity I observe. One reason is the human tendency to blame the other guy.

It will probably surprise many readers to learn that there's a social science term for this tendency to blame the other guy. It's called the fundamental attribution error. What it means is that humans tend to attribute the actions of others to personality characteristics without taking other factors into account. Most of the time that's an error.

Our tendency to blame the boss for poor group results without taking budgetary constraints, the lack of group member cooperation, or the lack of other necessary resources into account is an example of an attribution error. When we say that lack of upper management support is the reason for group failure, despite the fact that many group members don't even come to meetings and no one can agree when they do come, that's an attribution error. When members say that Harry is at fault because he just won't shut up despite the fact that no one else seems willing to talk, that's an attribution error.

Researchers have also uncovered general patterns in how individual group members interpret group success or failure. For example, leaders and powerful members tend to feel personally responsible for both group success and group failure. On the other hand, less powerful members take responsibility for group success but not for group failure. Instead, these members attribute group failure to leaders, powerful members, the organization, upper management, or other situational constraints.

People tend to misinterpret the behavior and motivation of others. This tendency to misinterpret increases conflict. When things aren't going well for the group, we are much more likely to blame others. Although the tendency to misjudge people, events, and actions is natural, it also has very negative effects on the group and on individuals who are wrongly judged.

For example, I often am called on to assist work groups that are mired in conflict and, as a result, are not within budget or time constraints or are not meeting target goals. There is usually a stable behavior pattern of attacks and counterattacks that has been going on for some time. My goal in working with such a group is to help the group free itself from this pattern and get back on track.

The problem confronting me in such a situation is that because the group is stuck in a pattern of conflict, members tend to focus on blaming outside forces, other members, or the leader for the group's predicament. As long as blaming is the primary pattern, the group will remain stuck. Also, the longer the blaming continues, the more powerless and frustrated group members will feel.

Changing a pattern of blame to one of collaboration and shared responsibility for group functioning and productivity is no easy task, however. Schein (1988), a well-known organizational consultant, wrote that the concept of teamwork is inconsistent with the U.S. emphasis on individualism and personal responsibility. Consequently, if the members accept shared responsibility for group function, each member will feel compelled to accept personal blame for group failure as well. Resistance to any information that disconfirms the belief that the group's problems are due to the actions of individual members, the leader, or authority figures external to the group is the inevitable result. Unless group members begin to see the situation differently, no change will occur.

One of the most powerful ways I have found to help members change their view of the situation is to talk with them about the normal human tendency to blame the other guy. Once members realize that they have made a mistake, they begin to look for other factors that are inhibiting progress. From that point on, changes happen fairly rapidly. Simply put, blaming is a symptom of a negative group pattern. Blaming is almost never a statement of fact. It is rare that one person is responsible for a group's problems. I believe that it is best to assume that is never the case, because that stops the blaming, which often leads the group in a positive direction.

Because I've heard it so many times before, I can almost hear some readers saying that, in their case, the leader really was to blame. Others are thinking it really was that member Harry's fault. Still others are thinking that upper management really was to blame.

I hear these statements so often it seems as if every leader, on every continent, is incompetent. I hear these statements so often that it seems as if every group, on every continent, contains an incompetent, evil, or mentally unbalanced member. This is simply not the case. Most groups contain people who are trying to do a good job. They may not know how. They may not be socially skilled, but they are trying.

My advice is to give everyone the benefit of the doubt not just for his or her sake but for your own and the group's sake. Blaming doesn't help. It only starts cycles of revenge and retaliation. Instead, find other factors that might be blocking group progress and fix them. Use the checklists in this book (for instance, the Effective Member Checklist at the end of this chapter) to help you determine other things to focus on. You'll be surprised at what happens when you do that. Things will start to get better.

By the way, I want to encourage people in management roles to start taking this advice as well. Stop replacing leaders or group members for alleged incompetence. Give teams the resources and training they need to work together effectively. Supply consultants, if necessary. All of us can make attribution errors, and the human cost of these errors is very high.

I had two reasons for starting this chapter by introducing the reader to the human tendency to blame the other guy. First, it pains me to repeatedly witness these misjudgments and their aftermath (e.g., transfers, firings, hurt feelings, and stress). Second, it means that all group members and leaders have responsibility for group success and group failings. The rest of the organization does also. Chapter 2 outlined what we know from research about how organizations can help the groups functioning within them. Chapter 6 will outline what leaders can do to help their groups be successful. This chapter outlines what members can do to help their group be successful. Everybody shares in the responsibility, and that's the truth.

Encourage the Process of Goal, Role, and Task Clarification

Encouraging the process of goal, role, and task clarification is simple to implement. All it means is that when you don't understand what's going on, ask questions until you do. It helps to ask questions of the group and not just the leader, because the discussion that follows will be richer and more likely to really clarify things for everyone.

Although this is a very simple thing to do, people hesitate to ask questions in the early stages of group development. This reticence is quite natural, but try to overcome it a little. Even if you ask only one question of the group, it will make a difference.

Many people have told me that they're afraid to ask questions for fear of being perceived as incompetent or naive. I am quite aware that image is seen as an important thing at work, but image is not everything. Even if image is very important, asking clarifying questions is unlikely to hurt your image. In fact, it may improve it. Others are most likely to see you as helpful, courageous, or down to earth for asking clarifying questions. None of those qualities is bad for your image.

Encourage the Adoption of an Open Communication Structure in Which All Member Input and Feedback Is Heard

It won't surprise most readers to learn that some people talk more than others during meetings. Of course, some people are just shy or have less need to be heard than others do. However, many talk less because they don't feel invited to speak. This has happened to most of us at one time or another. You go to the first meeting of a group, and few people talk to you. When you do say something, very few people respond to what you have said. If this has happened to you, think about the kind of group it was and the kind of people it contained. Was there anything about you that was different from others? Were you:

- one of the oldest in the group?
- one of the youngest in the group?
- new to the organization or group?
- one of only a few women in an otherwise male group?
- one of only a few men in an otherwise female group?
- the only one from your profession or area?
- one of only a few minorities in the group?

Were there any other obvious differences between you and other group members?

People tend to unconsciously classify others and assign high or low status to them based on external characteristics, especially during early meetings. Sometimes, it can be things as seemingly meaningless as height, clothes, mannerisms, and the like that get you classified into a high- or low-status position in a group.

By the way, people aren't bad when they classify others and assign them high or low status based on that classification. We all do it, all the time, sometimes without even being aware of what we're doing. In some cases, our tendency to do this can be very helpful. It can keep us out of harm's way. In work groups, however, our tendency to do this can be quite detrimental.

In the beginning of a group, communication patterns get established very quickly. Who talks to whom and who gets to talk a lot or a little become clear within a few meetings. No one talks about this; it just happens. The problem with this is that who talks to whom and who gets to talk a lot or a little are usually determined by status characteristics such as age, gender, ethnicity, and organizational position. Once a person is assigned a position in the food chain, it's hard to break out of it.

For example, women and minorities still tend to be assigned lower status in groups. As a result, they are expected to talk less, and they may be assigned less influential group roles. They often report dissatisfaction with their lower status, and other group members sometimes report uncertainty about the status of minority and female group members. Although this is beginning to change, we still have a long way to go before this tendency to assign lower status to members of certain groups is eradicated.

Group performance suffers when member role and status assignments are inappropriate or when member contributions are ignored. Potentially valuable contributions are overlooked, and goal achievement and productivity suffer as a result. Researchers have identified individual strategies and group conditions that increase the status of women and minorities in groups, however. These strategies may be helpful to any person whose group role or status is not commensurate with his or her abilities.

People who do not accept the lower status assigned to them increase the likelihood of improving their position in the group. People who act in group-oriented, as opposed to individual-oriented, ways tend to improve their group status as well. Also, people who demonstrate their competence and abilities to the group tend to increase their status, especially if they have enough time to demonstrate that competence. Eventually, other group members see these demonstrated abilities, and there is no longer a need for the person to prove his or her worth to the group.

Although research has focused mainly on women and minorities, the same advice works for anyone who is perceived as lower in status for whatever reason. On the individual level, the research suggests that the following strategies can help to elevate one's status in the group:

- Diplomatically resisting an inappropriate role assignment or status
- Demonstrating one's competence and abilities
- Acting in a cooperative, group-oriented way

On the group level, time aids the process of redefinition or reassignment of roles and changes in communication patterns. There's also another factor that helps tremendously. When all members take responsibility to ensure that everyone is heard from and that they are all clear about and comfortable with their roles, the chances of group success increase. Valuable input and skills will be used instead of lost.

Ensuring that everyone has the opportunity to be heard can be as simple as stopping periodically to check in with everyone. This takes only a few minutes but can make a big difference in group success.

Promote an Appropriate Ratio of Task Communications to Supportive Communications

In Chapter 3, I discussed the importance of supportive comments to group success. Statements focused on the group's work task are also very important, of course. If we engage only in supportive conversation, we may feel better but won't get much work done. Members of work teams that are successful spend between 70% and 80% of the time talking about goals and tasks. That means that out of 100 statements made by team members, 70 to 80 are work oriented. The next most common kind of statement made in high performance teams is supportive. The remainder are statements that express disagreement, focus on topics unrelated to the task, or express some form of dependency. If the proportion of these various kinds of statements changes very much, the group will be less successful.

What this means in practical terms is that when the group strays into an extended conversation about a football game, it is helpful to try to refocus the discussion on the task at hand. Likewise, if the group has been intensely discussing work tasks for an extended period of time, it might be helpful to compliment the group for its efforts or express support in some other way. Balance in group conversation, as in life, helps a lot.

Promote the Use of Effective Problem-Solving and Decision-Making Procedures

Before I discuss the process of problem solving and decision making, it is necessary to bring up an important question: Who should participate in solving problems and making decisions? Most organizations encourage workers at all levels to participate in these important processes. However, research suggests that not all employees are capable of contributing to the problem-solving or decision-making process. Some people simply are not interested in these processes, and others do not think they know enough to be of help. To solve problems, group members need expertise in the problem area, confidence in their ability to help solve the problem, knowledge and experience related to the problem, interest in participating, and problem-solving skills.

Effective methods for problem solving and decision making have been studied by a number of researchers. Their results overlap. For example, Shaw (1954), a social psychologist, stated that effective group problem solving and decision making consists of four steps:

1. Recognizing the problem

2. Diagnosing the problem

3. Making the decision

4. Accepting and implementing the decision

Others have outlined a process, similar to Shaw's, that includes the following:

1. An orientation phase

2. A discussion phase

3. A decision phase

4. An implementation phase

Each of these phases has significant impact on the quality of a group's solutions and its overall productivity. For example, during the orientation phase, it is helpful to avoid dwelling on the problem, because focusing on deficiencies may lead members to become defensive. Instead, it is useful to begin by discussing good solutions that have been effective and investigating solutions developed by teams in other organizations that have proved to be effective. This puts a positive spin on the process and may expand the group's solution options. Then the problem is defined and strategies are outlined for solving the problem. Strategies include such things as how to gain needed information about the problem, how to analyze the information, and how to make the final decision. Research tells us that groups that outline these strategies in advance are more successful than those that do not. Unfortunately, many groups spend little or no time planning strategies for problem solving and decision making. Some groups consider it a waste of time, even if members have been made aware of the fact that planning improves solution quality and group performance.

The amount of time spent discussing the problem and potential solutions increases the quality of the outcome. The amount of member participation in the discussion relates to the quality of the group's solution and overall effectiveness as well. Again, many groups do not spend adequate time discussing an issue. In some cases, a group will discuss only a few alternative solutions.

Groups can make the actual decision in a number of ways. The group may delegate the responsibility for the final decision to an individual, a subgroup, or an expert. Member inputs can be averaged to form the basis for a decision. Group members can vote on alternative proposals or may choose consensus as their decision-making method. Consensus refers to reaching a decision that is agreeable to all members. Efforts to determine which of these methods is best have been unsuccessful. People like the consensus method, but it doesn't necessarily produce better decisions. In general, people tend to like any method as long as they can live with the final decision. It is certain that participation in the decision-making process increases member satisfaction, however. It may also increase performance to some extent.

I want to insert a word of caution about using consensus inappropriately. In the last paragraph, I defined consensus as the process of reaching a decision that is agreeable to all members. This does not mean that all members would rate that proposed solution as their first choice. It simply means that they can live with that decision.

Many people think that consensus means that everyone must agree 100% with the proposal. If that is not the case, they believe, consensus has not been reached. This way of looking at consensus is very dangerous. If one person objects, the group cannot move forward. Viewed in this way, consensus is more like tyranny. One person can stop the group in its tracks. To avoid this potential pitfall, I recommend a modified version of consensus in which members assume that consensus exists if 70% to 80% of the members agree.

Implementing group decisions and evaluating those decisions are key elements in the process. Ideally, evaluation is built into the process, and the results of the evaluation form the basis for the group's next problem-solving process. Many of us have sat on committees and made recommendations that were never implemented. This is often the case when the group making the decision does not have the authority to implement its solution. Nothing is so demoralizing to a group. It is incumbent on the group, then, to interact with other groups that will be involved in implementation throughout its deliberations. This increases the likelihood of successful implementation of group decisions.

These findings suggest that problem solving and decision making are enhanced when groups outline, in advance, the strategies they will use to solve problems and make decisions. Discussing alternative solutions, ensuring implementation and evaluation, and involving all members in these processes are also associated with high quality problem solving and decision making.

Encourage the Establishment of Norms That Support Productivity, Innovation, and Freedom of Expression

You might be surprised at the number of groups I encounter that don't expect to generate the best possible product or result. I hear about what group members think they can get away with and about why time constraints, policies, and lack of resources will prevent the group from doing a good job. Although some of these constraints are very real, if a group agrees to mediocrity, that is what it will get. When groups agree to do the best possible job and to remove as many obstacles from their way as they can, excellence is the likely result.

Freedom of expression was discussed earlier when I advocated the development of an open communication structure. If members don't feel free to offer their ideas, it will be difficult for the group to be successful. In this section, I would like to add a few additional comments about freedom of expression.

Research on the effects of diversity on work group procedures and productivity has not led to unanimous conclusions. Some findings suggest that diversity improves work group performance, but other findings conclude that diversity has negative effects on performance. Surface-level differences, such as ethnicity, gender, race, and age, have been found to have negative effects on group processes and performance. Underlying differences, such as personality, education, and life experiences, do not have as much impact on work groups. Interpersonal conflicts have very harmful effects on groups, however. Whether those conflicts are instigated by diversity, personality, or gender, these conflicts can have very negative effects on work groups. Sometimes diversity increases interpersonal conflicts. However, diversity can also increase team learning, problem solving, and innovation.

It may be that the contradictions in research findings result from the significant increases in racial and ethnic diversity not only in the United States but also in countries all over the world. Social scientists are capturing glimpses of the rapidly changing makeup of populations across the globe and our efforts to become more inclusive.

In the meantime, what can work group members do to improve group performance and increase the participation of all members? Fortunately, the research is quite clear about one thing. Group members need to avoid interpersonal conflicts and embrace task conflicts. Functional differences among members, such as differences in expertise, background, and educational level, lead to task conflicts, which are necessary for effective problem solving, decision making, and high performance. If team members focus on the work and avoid interpersonal conflicts, diversity of all types becomes a resource. Members learn from each other, make better decisions, and improve group productivity and effectiveness. To benefit from diversity, everyone must be heard and involved in the discussion.

Go Along With Norms That Promote Group Effectiveness and Productivity

Norms are collective value judgments about how members should behave and what should be done in the group. Norms are necessary if group members are to coordinate their efforts and accomplish their goals. Establishing rules or norms about unimportant things or the wrong things has a chilling effect on groups, however. If individuals cannot express dissent, for example, things will not go well.

Sometimes norms get established about unimportant things. For example, I know of groups in which members are expected to eat lunch together every day. In other groups, members are expected to come to work at least an hour before work actually begins. Norms like these may inhibit individual freedom and cause resentment.

On the other hand, some degree of coordination and conformity is necessary for group success. It is important, then, to go along with norms that promote group effectiveness and productivity. Although you might prefer a different way of doing things, if the established norm is likely to work, conformity is advised.

Which norms encourage productivity? Research tells us that norms encouraging high performance standards and effectiveness increase team productivity. Shared expectations of success also support productivity. A norm that encourages innovation increases the likelihood of higher productivity as well. Norms and values that support superior quality, service, innovation, and attention to detail significantly increase team effectiveness and productivity. Make sure that your team has norms like these and does not create other norms that block effectiveness, and things will go well.

Promote Group Cohesion and Cooperation

The following are some of the positive effects of cohesion in groups:

- Increased conformity
- Increased group influence over its members
- Increased member satisfaction with the group
- Increased group integration
- Increased cooperation

Box 5.1   Group Therapy

I got a call from a group leader. He said his group was a mess. When I asked what was happening, he gave me a lengthy personality profile of each group member. He also told me how each person related to other members and who was feuding with whom. The group's problem was caused by a lack of clarity about goals and tasks. When these issues were straightened out, the "personality problems" went away. Psychoanalysis was not necessary.

Cooperation, which is facilitated by cohesion and shared goals, has many positive effects on group functioning. The characteristics of cooperative groups are as follows:

- More effective communication
- A friendlier group atmosphere

- Stronger individual desire to work on group tasks
- Stronger commitment to the group
- Greater division of labor
- Greater coordination of effort
- Greater productivity
- Increased trust and the development of lasting agreements
- Increased ability to resolve conflicts

A word of caution with regard to cohesion is appropriate at this point. High levels of cohesion, in conjunction with certain factors, can have negative effects. That is, a group can make poor or, in some cases, dangerous decisions due to an overriding wish to maintain unity and cohesion. This wish can lead the group to overlook other choices or courses of action. A cohesive group may be in danger of making a poor decision, a condition called "groupthink," in the following circumstances:

- When groups deliberate in isolation and do not report or check their conclusion with others outside the group, the possibility of poor decisions increases.
- If the group's leader controls the discussion and makes his or her positions clear from the outset, poor group decisions are more likely.
- When groups are faced with important and stressful decisions, they tend to decide quickly to reduce the stress. This often results in poor decisions.

Cohesion alone does not pose a threat. As long as a group stays connected with others outside the group and has an effective leader, high levels of cohesion will have many positive effects on group productivity. How, then, can group members promote cohesion? Research tells us that when goals and methods to reach those goals are clear, cohesion increases. Also, successful conflict resolution reduces individual fears of rejection and increases trust between members. A feeling of "we-ness," or cohesiveness, results. Finally, although it is rarely clear what causes what in an interacting system, increased communication is associated with increased cohesion and vice versa.

Notice that the research does not suggest that sharing personal feelings, developing personal friendships, socializing outside work, or similar things increase group cohesion. It is not necessary to know other group members on a personal level to promote cohesion. Working to increase goal clarity and communication should occur in the work group. Conflict resolution should as well.

Conflicts continue to occur throughout a group's life. In fact, group conflict is almost as common as group cooperation. One could conclude that conflict seriously impairs group cohesion. Although this can be the result, cohesion can also be increased by conflict. Although this sounds paradoxical, it is important to note that in any relationship, the freedom to be oneself and to disagree without fear of rejection or retribution increases, rather than decreases, cohesion and trust. Also, conflict provides energy to the group and allows clarification of group values, goals, and structures. All of these have been found to be associated with increased cohesion and trust. Cohesion and conflict are linked. You can't have one without the other, so to speak.

Of course, how conflict is dealt with is the crucial factor in determining its effect on cohesion. Inevitably, conflict is resolved. How it is resolved will determine whether group cohesion is positively or negatively affected. Six methods of conflict resolution have been described by a number of researchers:

- Imposition of the position of an individual or subgroup on other members
- Withdrawal of an individual or subgroup from the group
- Inaction, whereby one or both sides of a conflict do nothing to resolve the conflict
- Yielding, in which one side gives up its position
- Compromise, in which the parties find a solution somewhere between their respective positions
- Problem solving, in which the source of the conflict is located and a mutually agreeable solution is found

The first four solutions have many negative repercussions. Imposition can result in hostility and passive-aggressive behavior on the part of group members. Withdrawal threatens the life of the group and reduces its resources through member loss. Inaction can result in simmering discontent, apathy, or alienation. Yielding may also elicit alienation and covert hostility. Compromise can be viable if the resolution of the conflict seems reasonable and acceptable to all concerned. Problem solving gives the best results, however, because it requires the actual resolution of different perspectives and a new group conceptualization of the issues involved in the conflict.

Some groups navigate their conflicts well, and others disband or become dysfunctional by dealing with their differences ineffectively. What do successful teams do to promote positive conflict resolution? Members of successful teams communicate their views clearly and explicitly. They avoid generalizations and

Box 5.2   Intensive Teamwork

Intensive care teams at higher stages of development save more patients' lives than ICU teams at lower stages of development.

are specific in their communication. They talk about trust and cooperation during the discussion. Members also initially respond cooperatively to others who are behaving competitively. If others continue to respond competitively, successful group members demonstrate their willingness to compete by arguing their position. Although this sounds like an inappropriate strategy, research suggests that it may result in cooperation from others because not to do so would result in continued stress or personal losses. Sometimes, demonstrating a willingness to compete will bring about cooperation from others. Demonstrating a willingness to compete may also result in being viewed as a more formidable opponent.

All of these strategies help maintain a reasonable trust level, which allows negotiations to proceed. Negotiation is an important conflict resolution strategy. Seeking a mutually agreeable, or win-win, solution has been found to increase communication and cooperation. It also tends to reduce conflict by breaking it down into specific issues that can be dealt with one at a time.

Sometimes the intensity and depth of the conflict are too great to be solved by the group members themselves. In such cases, a third party can help resolve the conflict. Group and organizational consultants are often asked to assist groups that are stuck as a result of seemingly insurmountable conflicts. This can be a useful strategy for conflict resolution. However, third-party intervention should be sought only if all parties want the help and if the intensity of the conflict is high. This last-resort strategy requires willingness on the part of the group and skill on the part of the third party.

Effective Member Checklist

Please read the statements below. Circle the number that most accurately describes your response to the statement. Use the following key to respond to each statement.

1 = Disagree strongly

2 = Disagree to some extent

3 = Agree to some extent

4 = Agree strongly

Section I

1. I avoid blaming others for group problems.

      1   2   3   4

2. I assume that every group member is trying to do a good job.

      1   2   3   4

3. I treat people as individuals and don't make assumptions about them based on my preconceived notions about people like them.

      1   2   3   4

4. I do not get bogged down in interpersonal issues or personality conflicts.

      1   2   3   4

Section I score: _____

Section II

5. I encourage the process of goal, role, and task clarification.

      1   2   3   4

6. I encourage the use of effective problem-solving and decision-making procedures.

      1   2   3   4

7. I encourage the group to outline, in advance, the strategies that will be used to solve problems and make decisions.

      1   2   3   4

8. I work to ensure that decisions and solutions are implemented and evaluated.

      1   2   3   4

9. I encourage norms that support productivity, innovation, and freedom of expression.

      1   2   3   4

(Continued)

(Continued)

---

10. I encourage the use of effective conflict management strategies.

      1   2   3   4

11. I support the division of labor necessary to accomplish goals.

      1   2   3   4

Section II score: _____

Section III

12. I work to ensure that the input and feedback of every member is heard.

      1   2   3   4

13. I work to ensure that we all have a chance to demonstrate our competence and skills in the group.

      1   2   3   4

14. I discourage any group tendency to adopt excessive or unnecessary norms.

      1   2   3   4

15. I am, and encourage others to be, cooperative.

      1   2   3   4

16. In conflict situations, I communicate my views clearly and explicitly.

      1   2   3   4

17. I respond cooperatively to others who are behaving competitively.

      1   2   3   4

Section III score: _____

Section IV

18. I act, and encourage others to act, in the best interests of the group.

      1   2   3   4

19. When members contribute good ideas, I express my appreciation.

      1   2   3   4

20. I encourage and work to achieve mutually agreeable solutions to conflict.

      1   2   3   4

21. I support the leader's efforts to coordinate and facilitate group goal achievement.

      1   2   3   4

22. I offer advice to the leader when I think the advice will be helpful.

      1   2   3   4

Section IV score: _____

Section V

23. I have negotiated, or would be willing to negotiate, with other groups and individuals to help my group obtain needed resources.

      1   2   3   4

24. I share information and impressions I have about other parts of the organization with the group.

      1   2   3   4

25. I encourage the group not to overwhelm itself with too much external information or demands.

      1   2   3   4

26. I talk positively about my group to outsiders.

      1   2   3   4

27. I keep other members of the organization informed about what my group is doing.

      1   2   3   4

Section V score: _____

Section VI

28. When members stray off task, I diplomatically try to bring the discussion back to the task.

      1   2   3   4

29. I go along with norms that promote group effectiveness and productivity.

      1   2   3   4

30. I encourage high performance standards.

      1   2   3   4

(Continued)

(Continued)

31. I expect the group to be successful and productive.

| 1 | 2 | 3 | 4 |

32. I encourage innovative ideas.

| 1 | 2 | 3 | 4 |

33. I use what I have learned about group development and productivity to help my group become effective.

| 1 | 2 | 3 | 4 |

34. I encourage the group to frequently assess its functioning and alter it if necessary.

| 1 | 2 | 3 | 4 |

35. I volunteer to perform tasks that need to be done.

| 1 | 2 | 3 | 4 |

Section VI score: _____

Total minimum score: 35

Total maximum score: 140

My score: _____

What is your overall membership quotient?

Total Score	Your Membership Grade
126+	A
112–125	B
98–111	C

What are your section scores?

Section I: Attitudes and Feelings

Total Score	Your Grade
14+	A
12–13	B
10–11	C

Section II: Processes and Procedures

Total Score	Your Grade
25+	A
22–24	B
20–21	C

Section III: Communication and Participation

Total Score	Your Grade
22+	A
19–21	B
16–18	C

Section IV: Support and Encouragement

Total Score	Your Grade
18+	A
16–17	B
14–15	C

Section V: Intergroup Relations

Total Score	Your Grade
18+	A
16–17	B
14–15	C

Section VI: Work and Productivity

Total Score	Your Grade
29+	A
25–28	B
22–24	C

⊰ SIX ⊱

EFFECTIVE TEAM LEADERSHIP

———◆●◆———

The belief that leaders are instrumental in the creation of effective teams is deeply rooted in society and in the social sciences. Today's conceptions of leadership are not very different from the earliest views, which described leaders as people with special inborn characteristics that propelled them into leadership roles. Currently, although most social scientists reject the notion of inborn traits, many still see leadership as residing in the individual because it is assumed that people can learn how to be effective leaders by acquiring certain knowledge and skills. Hundreds of thousands of managers and executives have attended leadership training programs over the years in order to learn to be effective leaders. Now, most leaders have coaches as well.

Leaders are thought to facilitate the development of shared understanding and interpretations of reality among group members. They articulate things that haven't previously been explicitly stated that can provide new visions for the group. Inherent in this position is the assumption that the leadership role is vital to the creation and maintenance of an effective team. This assumption has led some researchers to study the cognitive capacities of leaders to determine how effective leaders think about their role. Again, the goal of such studies is to discover effective leadership styles that can then be taught to other leaders or potential leaders.

The old notion of the charismatic leader is experiencing a comeback. In this view, the leader is seen as the one who instills new thinking in followers and redirects group activities. These views of leadership support the assumption that leaders are central to the creation and redirection of group culture. In fact, leaders are perceived as having so much power that, should they act in selfish or unethical ways, great damage can be done to the group and its members. Leaders are clearly perceived as capable of making a significant difference in groups.

For the average person in a leadership role in the workplace, these views of leaders as crucial to group success can be overwhelming. It's all up to you when you're the leader. If the group fails, it's your fault. The stress of this enormous personal responsibility can have negative effects on potential and actual leaders. Potential leaders may choose not to become leaders, and actual leaders may suffer emotional or physical stress as a result of this sense of responsibility. Also, leaders worry about repercussions if their groups are perceived by upper management to be unproductive. Leaders know that they will be held accountable for the group's lack of productivity.

Some social scientists disagree with the prevailing, one-sided view of the leader as central to team effectiveness and success. Some emphasize the interdependence of leaders, followers, and the dynamic forces in which a group operates. In this view, all group members share responsibility for creating an effective team. Multiple discussions among all members eventually result in shared assumptions about goals and the methods needed to accomplish those goals. Leaders are part of this process but are not necessarily a primary part. Group success or failure is the result of many mutual influences.

Group development theories also suggest that a group's culture and structure are the products of processes inherent in groups. This view of the creation of effective teams is not as leader-centric. The creation of group culture is seen as the result of intrinsic forces. Consequently, the content of culture in different groups is not uniform. Rather, the particulars of a culture result from the resolution of differences and disagreements that emerge in that group. However, the process is the same from group to group, and all members are involved in the creation of a group's unique culture and structure.

Although minority opinions such as those just reviewed do exist, the majority view of leaders as key to group success dominates our thinking. In the current climate, the focus is on leaders, not members. In this chapter, I will try to reduce that focus a bit and decrease the overwhelming feeling of responsibility associated with leadership in today's work environment. I will present guidelines for what leaders can do to help their groups become effective and productive teams. As has been the case throughout this book, the guidelines are based on research. Inherent in these guidelines is an assumption of mine, which is that leaders alone cannot be held responsible for group success or failure. Having reviewed the leadership research, I am convinced that the view of groups as interdependent systems is the more accurate one. I have already alluded to this assumption in previous chapters. In fact, two of the preceding chapters could not have been written if I had believed that leaders are ultimately responsible for group outcomes. The larger organization, external conditions, and group members also influence group success or failure. Although leaders can help or hinder the process, so can members.

I also want to dispel the myth that leaders must be special people with a tremendous amount of skill in order to be effective. The average person of goodwill, who is flexible and willing to learn some basic skills, can be an effective leader. Not all situations require leaders of exceptional skill. In fact, in many group situations, charismatic leaders may inhibit group progress because their dominating presence may reduce member participation and motivation to take on certain tasks necessary for group success. Groups work well when all members actively participate. If leaders remain prominent throughout group life, groups will be less likely to succeed. With these assumptions as a foundation, the following guidelines for effective leadership are presented. As you read the rest of this chapter, think about a group that you are leading at the moment or have recently led. Ask yourself the following questions:

- Do I follow these guidelines?
- Can I think of examples of times when I exhibited these behaviors or attitudes?
- Can I think of times when I should have exhibited these behaviors or attitudes but, for some reason, did not?
- In what areas do I need to improve?
- What do I plan to do to improve in these areas?

There are certain things you must keep in mind and certain things you must do if you are going to be an effective team leader. The following guidelines outline how leaders become effective.

Don't Take On Every Leadership Assignment You Are Offered

Research attempts to determine the personal characteristics of effective leaders have a long and disappointing history. The search for leadership traits has not resulted in many consistent findings. Despite all the effort, only a few traits have been consistently identified. Effective leaders tend to have more task-related abilities, be more social, and be more motivated to be leaders than others.

Although these findings indicate that a few personal characteristics do influence leadership capabilities, it is important to note that task-related abilities will vary in different situations. The same is true of the kinds of social skills required of leaders in different situations. Therefore, the same person will not necessarily be an effective leader in every context.

An effective leader of an engineering product development team, for example, might be ineffective as a leader of a group in the financial or hotel industry. Although this may seem self-evident, in large organizations composed of many different businesses, people are often transferred between businesses without regard to task competence. Such transfers are based on the assumption that effective leaders will be effective in a variety of contexts and that knowledge of a group's task is not essential for leadership. Research suggests that this is not the case. To be effective, leaders must understand the work of a group.

The social skills needed in different leadership roles also vary. An outgoing, engaging, and charming style might be needed in some situations. In others, a more sedate, low-key style works best. Although some people may be able to adjust their styles to meet different social demands, others may not be as successful. All leaders must adjust their styles at different times in order to facilitate group progress. However, leaders should be aware that certain personality characteristics are difficult to change, and task competence in very different areas is difficult to come by. The bottom line, then, is that it is best to be selective about the leadership roles you take on. Choose to take on a leadership role when you understand the group's work and you believe that you will be able to meet group needs.

Adjust Your Leadership Style to Meet the Developmental Needs of the Group at a Particular Time

Member perceptions of the role of the leader change at different stages of group development. In Stage 1, the group perceives the leader as benevolent and powerful. She or he is perceived as the source of member safety and reward. In Stage 2, members begin to challenge the leader's authority and control. In order for the group to mature, such challenges are necessary. The role of the leader must be redefined if the group is to move into the more mature stages of development. When power is redistributed as groups mature, all group leaders experience some loss of influence and prominence.

Groups that successfully move through the developmental sequence do so in part by changing the relationship between members and the leader. The leader—once benevolent, then authoritarian in the eyes of members—emerges in later stages as a more realistic group facilitator and coordinator. Earlier mythic qualities ascribed to the leader by members are stripped away, and a human being with a job to do emerges. Leader prominence is less necessary in later stages of development because goals and roles have become clear. Members' roles have emerged that take over certain aspects of the leader's role. The elaborated group social structure makes leader prominence unnecessary and potentially disruptive. Leadership is still necessary for coordination; however, both leaders and members provide that coordination.

These changes in status and perceptions take their toll on the bravest of leaders. Because most people who assume a leadership role are not aware of these naturally occurring group processes, they may feel defeated as a result of attacks and challenges to their authority that occur in Stage 2. However, for the group to develop further, the leader's role must change significantly.

In mature and productive teams, members assume many of the functions that leaders performed at earlier stages. For this to occur, the leader's role must become less directive and more consultative. Leaders can help to redistribute power among members by altering their leadership style to match the needs of the group. This entails knowing what the needs of the group are at any given time and how to behave in order to facilitate movement.

In a way, leadership and parenting have a lot in common. An effective parent interacts differently with a small child than with that same child as an adolescent or a young adult. Maintaining one parenting style throughout the life of a child would be disastrous. Maintaining one style of leadership throughout the life of a group would be detrimental also. One style will not meet group needs and will not facilitate the development of an effective and productive team. The question for leaders, then, is, "What leadership style is best at the different stages of group development?" The following guidelines suggest ways for leaders to behave when groups are in the different stages of group development.

Leadership at Stage 1: Be a Directive and Confident Leader

In a new group, members expect leaders to be directive, confident, organized, and task oriented. Group members haven't had the time to organize themselves yet.

That will come later. In the meantime, members want the leader to provide that structure for them. Don't be afraid to do that. Many new leaders feel that it is best to ask members to help structure the group from the beginning. Although this may seem democratic and right, it tends to make members feel insecure and slows group progress.

Come into meetings with a clear, written agenda. State the group's goals as clearly as possible. Run meetings efficiently and assign tasks to individuals as necessary. If decisions are called for, make them. Your initial attempts to organize things will be modified later as group members become more involved. In the beginning, however, providing direction and appearing confident of group success are essential.

Work to Reduce Members' Anxiety, Fears of Rejection, and Concerns About Safety

In the first stage of group development, members' dependency, anxiety, and need for inclusion and safety are at their height. The leader is likely to be seen as benevolent, competent, and the provider of safety to anxious group members. One of the leader's main jobs during this time is to reduce the anxieties of group members. Leaders can reduce member anxiety by expressing confidence and providing direction. In addition, it is important to be fair and sensitive when dealing with members. Make sure that you don't put individuals on the spot or react negatively to anyone. Also, help members to feel included by addressing people by name and inviting members to participate. Initially, inviting participation is helpful. Insisting on participation or singling out nonparticipators is not helpful, however.

Provide Positive Feedback

In the beginning of a group, positive feedback from the leader increases cohesion. Using your leadership position to reward rather than punish members will facilitate group development. There are many ways to accomplish this. Thanking people for their attendance, input, and ideas is just one way to provide positive feedback.

Facilitate Open Discussion of Goals, Values, and Tasks

In the first stage of group development, leaders play an important role in facilitating group growth. This is because leaders have the most clearly defined role during this period. Because development is progressive, the task of a leader at Stage 1 is to facilitate movement to the next developmental phase. That is, the leader's task is to act in ways that will precipitate open discussion of values, goals, tasks, and leadership so that differences of opinion about these elements of group life can surface. This will move the group in the direction of Stage 2. Because people are hesitant to express different opinions at Stage 1, it is sometimes useful to ask people to express their views anonymously. This can be accomplished by asking people to write down their views on a specific issue. Next, those views can be summarized and shared with all members. This makes open discussion of divergent opinions much easier because no individual has to claim responsibility for expressing a difference of opinion or for being the first to disagree with a particular view.

Help Members Feel Competent by Providing Supervision, Training, and Education for Task- and Process-Related Activities

It is important for members to feel competent in relation to group goals and tasks. In some groups, members enter the group with great skill. However, skill levels may not be the same for all group members. It is helpful to review the skills necessary to accomplish the group's tasks with all members to ensure that everyone is on the same page.

Training in group participation skills is as important as training in task-related skills. Typically, group leaders have received much more training about groups than members have received. As stated earlier, hundreds of thousands of people have attended leadership training. I know of very few membership training seminars besides those that I conduct myself. The assumption seems to be that if leaders understand how groups operate, they will be able to make those groups and their members behave effectively. This is not the case. Members are vital to group success and need the same knowledge and skill about group participation that leaders need.

If certain necessary skills in the task or group participation area are lacking, then training, education, supervision, or a combination of these may be needed to ensure group success. Again, members are unlikely to ask for these things at this early stage of development. Therefore, it is incumbent on leaders to determine members' skill levels and which skills might need strengthening. Anonymous surveys or private interviews with group members may be helpful in this regard. Use the Effective Member Checklist in Chapter 5 to determine what group members need to learn. It would be helpful to ask members to read this book. They will learn not only about their role as members but also about your role as leader. That will make a big, and positive, difference.

Set High Performance Standards and Provide Guidance as Needed

Research tells us that groups with high performance standards tend to be more successful. Setting those standards from the beginning is very important. During discussions about goals, then, it is helpful not only to describe the product that the group is expected to generate but also to discuss expectations about the quality of that product. It is also helpful to review standards for group participation. Use the Effective Member Checklist in Chapter 5 and the Effective Leader Checklist in this chapter as ways of setting performance standards for member and leader participation.

Manage the External Environment for the Group

One of the important functions leaders must perform in the early stages of group development is managing the group's interaction with the rest of the organization. Later on, members will take over some aspects of this function. Initially, however, it falls to the leader to negotiate with other groups and individuals for needed resources, buffer the group from excessive external demands, and report on group progress as a way of ensuring that the group is regarded positively by the rest of the organization.

Leadership at Stage 2: When Members Begin to Demand More Participation in Running the Group, Slowly Begin to Empower Them

In the first stage of group development, leaders have great influence. Members tend to depend on the leader for direction and safety. Leaders have a good deal of influence with regard to initial definition of goals and preliminary decisions about the type of group structure being established. Group members expect the leader to provide direction, safety, order, and group goals and structures. Attempts to engage members in these activities at Stage 1 would be futile.

During Stage 2, however, member expectations and reactions to the leader change quite a bit. As members become more comfortable in the group, they begin to resent what they now perceive to be undue influence on the part of the leader. The leader's competence may be challenged. Some members may feel manipulated by the leader. The safety and competence that members perceived the leader as providing are questioned. Suspicion of and challenges to the leader's authority often begin to take place.

Not all members become disenchanted with the leader. Some remain loyal. The group may split into two factions over this issue. One faction is supportive of the leader and the other is not. These two factions often fight about their expectations of the leader and her or his performance with regard to those expectations. Some of this conflict may be due to actual leader behavior in the group. Much of the conflict is about things that go beyond the role of the leader, however. In essence, the conflict with and about the leader is a way for the group to discuss who can have input into decisions. Roles and decision making, power, status, and communication structures are being clarified in this process. Efforts to redistribute power begin to occur as well. This is all necessary for group progress.

During the first stage of group development, the role of leader is the most differentiated and important role. Other roles are just being assigned. The leader role is necessary to the establishment of some sense of safety and order. In effect, the role of leader and members' reactions to that role are the impetus for the emergence of other roles and structures in the group. The prominence of the leader at Stage 1 and member dependence on the leader allow initial structures to form. Once these are in place, the group can begin to define its structure even further. A major way that the group does this is by redefining the leader's role and reducing, to some extent, the power associated with that role. This redistribution of power clears the way for other structures and roles to emerge.

So far, this seems like a reasonable and natural transition. However, leaders have used their power during Stage 1. The acquisition of power tends to make people want more power, not less. Thus, the redistribution of power necessary for further group development is not an easy process. When leaders meet resistance, their efforts to exert power and influence tend to increase, not decrease.

Three types of power have been described in the literature. There is power over, which is associated with dominance. Power from is the ability to resist unwanted influence and demands. Power to, or empowerment, is the ability to act more freely through power sharing. The strategies of power over and power from tend to have negative effects on group relationships and goal achievement. Such leadership tactics often push others to attempt to take power from the leader, and conflict is the inevitable result. Leaders who use power to, or empowering, strategies facilitate group development because no leader can perform all the functions of leadership alone. Redistribution of power is essential to group development and productivity.

Box 6.1   From Dead Birds to the Newsroom

She was the leader of specialists working to find ways to prevent birds from flying into airplane engines. She was so effective as a leader that the corporation, which had acquired many enterprises, transferred her to become the leader of a network newsroom.

Given the previous discussion, a group is not always successful in altering its perceptions, or the leader's perceptions, of the leadership role. Also, even if the group's perceptions change, the leader may force or coerce the group into continuing to respond as it did in Stage 1. Should the group fail to alter its perceptions, it will regress to the dependency stage of group development. Should the leader and group disagree about the leader's role and be unable to resolve this controversy, a prolonged fight for power and control is likely to occur. The group will then remain in Stage 2 for an extended period of time. Should that happen, the group's cohesiveness, social structure, and productivity will be adversely affected. Power struggles, fights, and the like will take precedence over goal achievement, efficiency, and productivity.

Effective leaders expect challenges to their authority and expect member demands for more participation in running the group. These leaders see those challenges and demands as a positive sign of group progress and not as threats to their authority. They respond to these challenges by slowly beginning to empower group members to participate more equally in group management functions. Effective leaders do this slowly, because it will take members some time to work out conflicts and roles with regard to group management. Giving up the reins all at once could be disruptive. A slower redistribution of power will be most effective.

Don't Take Attacks and Challenges Personally

One of the reasons why groups fail to resolve the tension and conflict inherent in this stage of group development is that leaders and members tend to personalize the experience. That is, when others challenge an individual member's views, the member has a natural tendency to feel hurt and personally attacked. Leaders who are attacked or discounted by members also tend to perceive these incidents as personal affronts. As a result, people may become quite defensive or combative. This escalation of tension to unmanageable levels may significantly reduce the group's chances of resolving conflict and creating a unified group culture and structure.

Adopting a group perspective can be very helpful to members and leaders, especially at this stage. If the events of Stage 2 are viewed from this perspective, they are understood very differently. Rather than feeling personally attacked, a leader with a group perspective could view the attack as a sign that the group is ready to define its structure further. The leader would view her or his role at this stage as a focus or catalyst for continued development. She or he would not feel threatened by the loss of some power or influence. Rather, the leader might come to view this redistribution of power, roles, and tasks as essential to group productivity and goal achievement.

In like fashion, a member whose views are challenged by others could see the challenges as necessary to the establishment of shared goals and an integrated group culture and social structure. Instead of reacting defensively, the member might focus on clarifying her or his views and the views of others in an attempt to gain consensus. A group perspective makes it possible for people to view conflict as normal and necessary at this stage of group development.

In real situations, on numerous occasions, I have seen the positive effects of adopting a group perspective. If a group that is stuck in the conflict stage can adopt a group perspective, it may be able to free itself and move to higher developmental stages. The first step, then, is learning about group development and dynamics. Simply knowing about these phenomena is not enough, however. Leaders and members must be able to give up blaming each other in order to begin to resolve the conflicts. This is not easy. Even though we know intellectually that conflict, attacks, and disagreements are normal and necessary parts of group development, on an emotional level we may feel hurt or angry. Our emotions may overwhelm us and lead us to seek revenge or vindication rather than reconciliation and consensus. In many cases, group members and leaders would rather get even than succeed.

**Act in Ways That Facilitate Open Discussion and Resolution
of Conflicts Regarding Values, Goals, and Leadership**

Conflict resolution increases group cohesion and trust, which makes it possible for the group to focus on strategies to achieve shared goals. In short, it moves the group toward the third stage of group development. Some strategies to manage conflict were discussed in the previous chapter. They are briefly outlined again here because both members and leaders have responsibility for discussion and resolution of conflicts.

Leaders and members of successful teams communicate their views clearly and explicitly. They avoid generalizations and are specific in their communication. They talk about trust and cooperation during the discussion. Leaders and members also initially respond cooperatively to others who are behaving competitively. If others continue to respond competitively, successful group leaders and members demonstrate their willingness to compete by arguing their position.

Negotiation is an important conflict resolution strategy. Seeking a mutually agreeable solution has been found to increase communication and cooperation. It also tends to reduce the conflict by breaking down the problem into specific issues that can be dealt with one at a time.

When the intensity and depth of the conflict are too great to be solved by the group members themselves, a third party can help resolve the conflict. Third-party interventions should be sought only if all parties want the help and if the intensity of the conflict is high. This last-resort strategy requires willingness on the part of the group and skill on the part of the third party.

Leadership at Stage 3:
Involve Members in the Leadership Function

Involving members as participants in the leadership process is the hallmark of Stage 3 leadership. Because leaders cannot perform every task, delegation and power sharing are necessary and indicative of an effective leadership style at this stage.

Leader prominence is less necessary at later stages of development because goals and roles have become clear. Member roles have emerged that take over aspects of the leader's role. The elaborated group structure makes leader prominence unnecessary and potentially disruptive. The leader moves into a more consultative role with the group. Leadership is still necessary for coordination; however, that coordination function is now shared by members and the leader. The following guidelines describe what effective leaders do at Stage 3.

Encourage and Support Members' Efforts to Share in the Leadership Function

In Stage 3, members are ready to facilitate meetings or portions of meetings. By this time, they are capable of working in subgroups to accomplish goals. Members will be giving reports about subgroup meetings and about tasks that have been accomplished between meetings. They will be involved in decision making and conflict resolution. Members will also be involved in negotiation, scanning, buffering, and group image and profile management within the larger organization. In short, members will have assumed many of the functions that were performed solely by the leader at earlier stages of development.

The leader is freed up to act more as a consultant to and supporter of members. The tasks of leaders and members of Stage 3 groups are the same. By this time, the power difference between leaders and followers has been reduced, and participants are operating in more egalitarian ways. All participants share equal responsibility for and commitment to the group. Their shared task is to consolidate gains in trust and cohesion and to organize themselves in ways that will ensure group productivity. Leaders who support, compliment, and praise members' efforts to share in the leadership function will increase the likelihood of group success.

Encourage the Group to Make Any Necessary Changes in the Group's Structure to Facilitate Group Productivity

One of the primary tasks of a Stage 3 group is to assess how it is functioning and to make any adjustments that will facilitate group productivity. Leaders encourage members to do this but do not do the work for the group. Instead, they provide ways for members to identify issues that may impede productivity and to determine ways to remove those impediments. They also participate, along with members, in identifying impediments to group success and in planning strategies to overcome those impediments. The checklists in previous chapters could be used as one way to approach this task.

Leadership at Stage 4: Participate as an Expert Member of Your Team

Leaders of Stage 4 teams can relax a little bit. Things should be going pretty smoothly. Members have taken on responsibilities and are actively pursuing group goal achievement. Leaders continue to act as consultants, as needed. In general, however, they participate along with members in achieving objectives and team success.

Continue to Monitor Team Processes, Especially for Signs of Regression

Each time a member leaves, new tasks are added, external conditions change, or other factors shift in some significant way, team dynamics are affected. In each of these circumstances, the team will experience disruptions, and adjustments will be needed to regain former levels of cohesion and productivity. Awareness and discussion of this fact of team life on the part of leaders and members is essential. Leaders and members can help maintain team effectiveness by periodically assessing the team and identifying issues that must be addressed. In this way, a team can continually monitor its functioning and make necessary adjustments. Ways to conduct these periodic assessments are described in Chapter 10.

No team or individual sustains high levels of productivity for long periods of time. People and groups need periods of rest, relaxation, flight, grumpiness, and fun. Unrealistic expectations of our human capacities may be one of the biggest threats to individual and team effectiveness.

Conduct Organizational Support Reviews Regularly

In Chapter 2, the importance of organizational support to team success was discussed. I recommended that relevant external individuals and groups meet with the team on a regular basis to assess the adequacy of that organizational support and to plan ways to increase the level of support, if necessary. I encourage leaders to ensure that these reviews happen regularly throughout the life of the group. The frequency of reviews will vary from group to group, depending on the time frame allotted to the group to accomplish its work. For example, if a product development group has 18 months to accomplish its goal, I suggest a review at the very beginning, one about three months later, and then reviews at longer intervals. Do what makes sense for your group.

**Regardless of the Stage of Your Group,
Be an Effective Group Member**

Leaders also must be effective group members. Review the Effective Member Checklist in Chapter 5 to assess how well you are doing in that regard. Also, review the Effective Leader Checklist provided next to assess how well you are doing in your current leadership role.

Effective Leader Checklist

Please read the statements below. Circle the number that most accurately describes your response to the statement. Use the following key to respond to each statement.

1 = Disagree strongly

2 = Disagree to some extent

3 = Agree to some extent

4 = Agree strongly

Section I

1. I avoid taking leadership assignments for which I do not have sufficient task-related knowledge.

    1   2   3   4

2. I avoid taking leadership assignments for which I do not have the appropriate personal style.

    1   2   3   4

3. I am motivated to act as the leader of this group.

    1   2   3   4

4. I am able to adjust my leadership style to meet the developmental needs of the group at a particular point in time.

    1   2   3   4

5. I treat members sensitively and fairly.

    1   2   3   4

6. I give lots of positive feedback to the group and to individuals.

    1   2   3   4

7. I facilitate member feelings of competence by providing supervision, training, and education for task-related skills when necessary.

    1   2   3   4

8. I facilitate member feelings of competence by providing supervision, training, and education for group participation skills when necessary.

    1   2   3   4

9. I set high performance standards from the beginning.

    1   2   3   4

10. I review quality expectations early and often.

    1   2   3   4

11. I review standards for member and leader participation as well.

    1   2   3   4

12. Regardless of the group's stage of development, I follow the guidelines for effective group membership and the guidelines for effective leadership.

    1   2   3   4

Section I score: _____

Section II

13. With a Stage 1 group, I am a directive and confident leader.

    1   2   3   4

14. I come to early meetings with a clear, written agenda.

    1   2   3   4

15. At early meetings, I am able to state the group's goals clearly.

    1   2   3   4

16. Especially in the beginning, I run meetings efficiently.

    1   2   3   4

17. Early on, I am comfortable assigning tasks to individuals as necessary.

    1   2   3   4

(Continued)

(Continued)

---

18. Early on, I am comfortable making decisions as needed.

  1   2   3   4

19. In early meetings, I work to reduce member anxiety, fears of rejection, and concerns about safety.

  1   2   3   4

20. I address members by name and make sure members know each other's names from the beginning.

  1   2   3   4

21. I try not to put individuals on the spot, especially in early meetings.

  1   2   3   4

22. I encourage participation, but I don't demand participation.

  1   2   3   4

Section II score: _____

Section III

23. I facilitate open discussion of group goals, values, and tasks.

  1   2   3   4

24. I encourage the expression of different points of view.

  1   2   3   4

25. When members are having difficulty expressing different opinions, I use methods to elicit their opinions anonymously.

  1   2   3   4

26. When members begin to demand more participation in running the group, I slowly begin to empower them to do so.

  1   2   3   4

27. I expect challenges to my authority and see them as a sign of group progress.

  1   2   3   4

28. I try not to take attacks and challenges personally.

  1   2   3   4

29. I facilitate open discussion and resolution of conflicts that emerge.

  1   2   3   4

30. I encourage the use of effective conflict resolution strategies.

    1   2   3   4

Section III score: _____

Section IV

31. As the group matures, I increasingly involve members in the leadership function of the group.

    1   2   3   4

32. As the group matures, I encourage and support member efforts to share in the leadership function.

    1   2   3   4

33. As the group matures, I encourage the group to make any necessary changes in the group's structure to facilitate productivity.

    1   2   3   4

34. When a team is fully functional, I act more as an expert member than as a leader.

    1   2   3   4

35. When a team is fully functional, I continue to monitor team processes, especially for signs of regression.

    1   2   3   4

Section IV score: _____

Section V

36. Initially, I negotiate with external groups and individuals for needed resources.

    1   2   3   4

37. Initially, I buffer the group from excessive external demands.

    1   2   3   4

38. I scan the rest of the organization to collect information that might be useful to the group.

    1   2   3   4

(Continued)

(Continued)

39. I report group progress to others to ensure that the rest of the organization has a positive image of the group.

      1   2   3   4

40. I ask the organization to review its level of support for the team on
a regular basis.

      1   2   3   4

Section V score: _____

Total minimum score: 40

Total maximum score: 160

My score: _____

What is your overall leadership quotient?

Total Score	Your Leadership Grade
144+	A
128–143	B
112–127	C

What are your section scores?

Section I: General Leadership Attitudes and Skills

Total Score	Your Grade
47+	A
42–46	B
36–41	C

Section II: Stage 1 Leadership

Total Score	Your Grade
36+	A
32–35	B
28–31	C

Section III: Stage 2 Leadership

Total Score	Your Grade
29+	A
25–28	B
22–24	C

Section IV: Stage 3 and Stage 4 Leadership

Total Score	Your Grade
18+	A
16–17	B
14–15	C

Section V: Intergroup Leadership

Total Score	Your Grade
18+	A
16–17	B
14–15	C

SEVEN

NAVIGATING STAGE 1

Goals of Stage 1

Certain behaviors are characteristic of all beginning, or Stage 1, groups. These behaviors can be classified into three categories: concerns about safety and inclusion, member dependency on the designated leader, and a wish for order and structure. Because these categories of behavior happen in all groups during the dependency and inclusion stage, there must be a reason, or purpose, for their occurrence. If the overall goal of group development is to create an organized unit capable of working effectively and productively to achieve specific ends, then each stage of group development contributes to that overall goal in some way. The first step to achieving that overall goal is to create a sense of belonging and the beginnings of predictable patterns of interaction. That is the purpose of Stage 1.

By the end of Stage 1, members should feel a sense of loyalty to the group. They should want to belong to the group, and they should feel safe enough to contribute ideas and suggestions that will, in their opinion, help the group to achieve its overall objectives. If they don't, the group is likely to disintegrate or stagnate. Groups disintegrate when members stop attending meetings or participating in group-related activities between meetings. Groups stagnate when the group system fails to grow and mature.

This chapter describes events that typically happen during Stage 1 and what members and leaders can do to increase the likelihood that group members will emerge from Stage 1 with a sense of belonging and a feeling of safety. Also, through the efforts of members and leaders, the group will have developed rudimentary structures that provide an initial sense of order and predictability.

Box 7.1   Best Excuse

This group ran the company. The members were the senior vice presidents and the CEO. I was going over the results of a group assessment I had done with them. The group was stuck in Stage 1. Although they knew they disagreed about many things, no one was willing to raise controversial issues. In fact, many members didn't talk very much at meetings. I told them that things wouldn't change unless they began to discuss these things. The CEO said, "Oh, we forgot to tell you that we took the Myers-Briggs test and all of us scored high on introversion. We're all introverts." I replied, "I don't care if you're aardvarks. You guys run the show. Your cars cost more than people's homes. You have to talk to each other."

Concerns About Safety and Inclusion

The behaviors, feelings, and attitudes that members of new groups express can be summarized as follows:

- Members are concerned with personal safety in the group
- Members want to be accepted by other members and the leader
- Members fear rejection
- Members communicate in tentative and very polite ways

Here is an example of how concerns for safety and inclusion might occur in a new group:

You have been assigned to work on a new group. The first meeting is to be held at 10:00. People begin to arrive a few minutes before 10. You have decided to check things out during this meeting. After all, you know only two people in the room. You smile at a few people and they smile back, but there's not much talking going on. You feel a little awkward, and it's obvious that others do, too. A brave soul asks the person sitting next to him what the purpose of this team is going to be. She shrugs her shoulders in response. A couple of folks smile and giggle a bit. Someone says, "Adam told me something about it, but I'm not very clear on it. He just said that he was putting a group together to work on a new project, and he wanted me on the team." Another person says, "That's how it was with me, too." Others nod in agreement, and the room falls silent again.

What You Can Do

Now that you know that one of the goals of the first stage of group development is to create a sense of safety and inclusion, there are some things you can do in a situation like this one to help the group achieve that goal. For example, you can introduce yourself to the person next to you and talk about what you do in the organization. If you do this loudly enough, others may introduce themselves as well. If not, ask other people who they are.

When the room falls silent, you can comment on how first meetings are always a little awkward, but it usually gets better pretty quickly. Statements like these tend to make others feel more comfortable and stimulate further conversation. The key is to keep the goal in mind (safety and inclusion) and act in ways that increase the likelihood of achieving that goal. Don't wait for others to act. Don't wait for the leader to act. Remember that everyone is responsible for the achievement of group goals. So just do it.

Dependency on the Designated Leader

- The members express a need for dependable and directive leadership
- The leader is seen as benevolent and competent
- The leader is expected and encouraged to provide members with direction and personal safety
- The leader is very rarely challenged
- Cohesion and commitment to the group are based on identification with the leader

Here is an example of how these issues might occur in a new group:

After a few minutes, Adam arrives. He stops to greet a few people as he walks into the room. Everyone seems grateful for his arrival. You think to yourself that Adam is the designated leader of this new group, and he will get the ball rolling. Just his arrival seems to have made a difference. People seem more relaxed already. They are all looking at Adam, smiling, and waiting for him to speak.

Adam doesn't waste any time. He doesn't even ask people to introduce themselves. Because he knows everyone, he assumes that the others know each other as well. Instead, he begins to outline the tasks of the group and the timeline in which tasks have to be accomplished. Some people begin to look a little confused, and others seem a bit tense. No one says anything, though.

What You Can Do

At this time, dependence on the leader is normal. Members expect Adam to take charge. You don't want to undermine Adam's authority or credibility at this point, but you do want to help him do a good job. Adam has forgotten to do a few things. In the best of all possible worlds, Adam would have introduced himself and asked others to do the same. He would have stated the agenda of the meeting and handed out copies of that agenda. He would have stated the goal of the group and launched a discussion about that goal.

If you are the leader of a new group, don't make Adam's mistakes. Come to the meeting prepared. Make sure that people are introduced in enough depth so that they learn not just each other's names but also what everyone does and what they do well. Provide a detailed agenda that includes a written statement of the group's goal. Spend the first meeting discussing that goal.

Because Adam forgot to do those things, you as a member could help him and the group by asking him for introductions. It helps to say something like, "Adam, I may be the only one, but I don't know everybody. Can we introduce ourselves before we get started?"

In a similar fashion, you might ask what the agenda of the meeting is and ask for clarification of the group's goal. Usually, you won't have to ask all these questions. Others will chime in once the ice is broken. The key is to keep this goal in mind as well. At this point, the group needs a dependable, directive, and competent leader. Help Adam to meet that group need.

If you are the leader and members ask questions, make suggestions, or point out things that you have forgotten to do, thank them for their help. Don't get defensive or embarrassed, even if a member says something in a way that seems rude or challenging. Assume that group members are trying to be helpful and encourage them to participate. In the long run, you'll be happy that you did.

Some groups don't have designated leaders. This can be a problem that can slow group progress. If this is the case in your group, suggest that a group coordinator be chosen. Research suggests that leaderless groups have more difficulty getting organized and more difficulty progressing through the stages of group development.

A Wish for Order and Structure

- Goals are not clear to members, but clarification is not sought
- Members rarely express disagreement with initial group goals

- Group members assume that consensus about goals exists
- Role assignments tend to be based on external status, first impressions, and initial self-presentation rather than on matching member competencies with goal and task requirements
- Member compliance is high
- Communication tends to go through the leader
- Participation is generally limited to a few vocal members
- Conflict is minimal
- Conformity is high
- A lack of group structure and organization is evident
- Member deviation from emerging norms is rare
- Subgroups and coalitions are rare

Here is an example of how these issues might occur in a new group:

Adam responds to your request and states the goal of the group. He asks whether people are clear about the goal, and everyone nods. You remain a little confused by the goal, but because everyone seems to understand what's expected, you don't say anything. Next, Adam returns to outlining the tasks of the group and the timeline in which tasks have to be accomplished. He asks for volunteers to take on the various tasks.

What You Can Do

From reading this book, you know that if goals are not perfectly clear and accepted by everybody, the chances of group success are limited. You also know that planning how to accomplish tasks and discussing who should do each task are crucial to group success.

Finally, you know that ensuring that input is sought from all group members increases the chances of group success. So you ask Adam and the group members to discuss their understanding of the goal in a little more depth. Later, you raise the issue of role assignments. It's best to raise this issue by inquiring about your own role, especially if it doesn't seem appropriate to you based on your skills and abilities. Of course, chances are slim that you will have to raise all these issues. By now, other members will be raising issues as well.

A word of advice for leaders is in order here. You know that discussing goals at length, spending time planning how to accomplish tasks, and assigning tasks based on member skills are important to group success. Make sure these things happen, but don't hog the limelight. Having members raise issues, rather than raising all of these issues yourself, is a good thing. Don't be too perfect, and don't be too dominant. Provide for member safety. Provide initial direction and support members' attempts to participate.

This chapter has provided some examples of events that typically occur in Stage 1 groups. It is not meant to cover all possible scenarios. The real intention of this chapter and those that follow is to help members and leaders develop a framework to guide their actions in groups. The framework is pretty simple: Know the goals of each stage of development and act in ways that will help your group achieve those goals. If the members and leaders described in this chapter follow that advice, the group will move forward. Everyone will develop a sense of belonging and safety, members will begin to trust Adam's leadership skills, and the beginnings of order will appear. The group will be ready to move on.

EIGHT

SURVIVING STAGE 2

Goals of Stage 2

Having safely navigated the first stage of group development, members and the leader have developed an initial sense of loyalty to the group. Some degree of organization has begun to emerge, and people feel safer about speaking up in the group. Now, some hard work has to be done. If the group is to become a unit capable of performing at high levels, then both members and the leader need to create a unified group culture and an effective organizational structure in which to work.

Group culture is a set of shared perceptions or assumptions about values, norms, and goals. These assumptions, once established, dictate how people will behave and the kind of organizational structure the group will need in order to express its cultural assumptions and achieve its goals.

In the first stage of group development, members were concerned primarily about personal safety and feeling included. Preliminary discussions probably revolved around how people should interact in the group and how members should organize themselves to accomplish tasks. More discussion will be needed to reach agreement about these things, however. Every member will have to participate for this to occur.

The second stage of group development is described as a period of counterdependency and fighting. This is because conflict with the leader and among group members is inevitable if the goals of Stage 2 are to be reached. The group's goal at this stage is to develop a unified set of goals, values, and operational procedures, and this goal usually generates conflict. Differences of opinion are very likely to occur. Conflict is also necessary for establishing a trusting climate in which members feel free to disagree with each other.

Some groups become mired in conflict and remain stuck at this developmental stage. Other groups are overwhelmed by the stress of this phase and revert to leader dependence in an attempt to avoid further conflict. Neither of these outcomes has positive effects for the group or for the quality of work that will be generated by the group. Only through conflict resolution and the development of a unified view of the group's purpose and processes can true collaboration be achieved.

This chapter briefly describes typical events that happen during Stage 2 and what members and leaders can do to increase the likelihood that group members will emerge from this stage with a shared culture and an organizational structure that will enable them to be productive and successful. It also describes how working to achieve the goals of Stage 2 increases trust among group members and makes working together more enjoyable and more effective.

Creating a Unified Group Culture

The first thing a group needs to do during Stage 2 is to begin to create a unified group culture. Here are some things that happen as a group attempts to do this:

- Conflicts about values emerge
- Disagreements about goals and tasks emerge
- Increased feelings of safety allow dissent to occur
- Members challenge the leader and each other
- Clarification of goals begins
- Decreased conformity begins
- Deviation from emerging group norms begins

Here is an example of how these issues might occur in a Stage 2 group:

The group has been meeting for about eight weeks. Nina, the group's leader, is going over a list of things that the group needs to work on in the coming weeks if they are to stay on schedule. Suddenly, Jack says, "I'm not sure about this, Nina. How can they expect us to come up with such a complicated policy in such a short period of time? I'm not even sure that a policy will solve this problem. I'm not convinced this is the right way to go." A few other members nod their heads in agreement with Jack.

Nina is stunned. She thought that members had agreed to the group's goal weeks ago. She wonders whether this is just a power play on Jack's part or whether he really means it.

What You Can Do

This kind of situation occurs quite often in Stage 2 groups. When people say that the group seems to be going in circles or rehashing topics that have already been discussed and resolved, it is usually due to situations like this one. People are in a hurry to get on with business. They easily get upset with members who revisit issues that they think have been decided already.

Instead of getting frustrated or angry with an individual or two, try to remember two things. First, remember that when things were initially discussed, the group was in Stage 1. Some people didn't feel safe enough to express disagreement at that point. It seemed like everyone agreed, but not everyone expressed her or his opinion. Later on, when feelings of safety have increased, disagreements can be voiced. This is a good thing.

Second, when a group is faced with a complicated set of goals and tasks, it takes people some time to examine those goals and tasks thoroughly. Opinions can't be formed quickly, especially if those opinions are important to individual and group success. It's a good thing to revisit issues after members have had time to think. It's a very good thing, actually. Decisions or agreements made in haste often end up being the wrong ones.

To help the group, you could say something like, "I'm glad Jack brought this up. It makes a lot of sense to discuss our goals and objectives again to make sure everybody's on the same page." Whether you're a member or the leader of this group, this is a very helpful thing to say. It may be harder for Nina, as the leader, to say it because she may think Jack's comments were meant as an attack on her leadership. It would be wise of her to say it anyway. If Nina doesn't say it, a member should try to ward off a potentially negative argument between these two people. The issue isn't whether Jack is trying to undermine Nina's authority; he may or may not be doing that. It doesn't matter. What matters for the group at this stage in its development is to make sure that everyone agrees with and understands the group's goal.

Let's look at another example:

The group had developed the habit of holding lunch meetings. Jane didn't like this because she usually worked out at the company's gym during lunch. She skipped a meeting and went to the gym. Other members were appalled and confronted her about her lack of commitment to the group at the next meeting. Jane said that she didn't like the meeting time because it infringed on her personal time. She even said she bet that some other people were unhappy with the meeting time, too. A couple of people said they agreed with Jane. Some people just shook their heads.

What You Can Do

During Stage 1, many norms get established without much discussion. In this case, it is likely that meeting during lunch worked well for the group leader. In Stage 1, people tend to go along with whatever the leader proposes, so lunchtime meetings became the norm. As the group developed and people began to feel more comfortable with each other, those who didn't like the meeting time became more vocal. This, too, is a good thing.

If group norms undermine people's motivation to attend or participate in the group, changes are in order. Finding a mutually agreeable meeting time in a busy workplace is challenging. It's important, though. If members skip meetings, the effects on the group will be negative. A large part of each meeting will be devoted to catching people up on what occurred at the last meeting. This will slow down or stop group progress. If people attend but are resentful of the meeting time, they won't participate fully and may act in unproductive ways.

If a situation like this occurs in your group, it would be helpful to say something like this: "I think we should try to find a meeting time that fits everyone's schedule. How's Tuesday at 3?"

Many norms emerge during the first stage of group development that will be challenged in the second stage. Here is an example of how this might happen:

Lora tends to go on and on at meetings. Whatever the topic, she has an opinion, which she expresses in great detail. You want to express an opinion as well, and you know that other people would like to air their views. No one interrupts Lora, however. Everyone just sits and fidgets or stares straight ahead. No one feels that she or he can give feedback to others about their

group behavior. Although it's never been voiced, everyone knows that giving
feedback violates some unstated rule. Members feel that they have to be nice
and that they have to be tolerant in this group.

What You Can Do

Generally speaking, being nice and tolerant of others is a good norm to establish. If that means that the group will fail to achieve its work goals, however, then the norm is too strict and should be altered. As people begin to feel safer, voicing disagreement with norms and suggesting elimination or alteration of some norms will occur. In fact, it must occur if the group is to develop a culture that will support group goal achievement.

In this case, you could say something like the following: "Lora, I think I understand your position on this, and I want to hear from others as well before I make up my mind. What do the rest of you think about this?" You'll probably feel a little uncomfortable doing this because you're breaking a group rule. Keep in mind, though, that if Lora is allowed to monopolize the conversation for much longer, the frustrations of others will continue to mount. Eventually, someone (maybe even you) will explode and confront Lora in a very negative way. The confrontation may get very personal and precipitate a feud in the group. Some members will rush to Lora's defense, and others may join the attack against Lora. This not only will be a colossal waste of group time but will also be very hurtful to Lora and to group morale. It's better to intervene early in a situation like this. Do so with all the diplomacy and tact you can muster. Be gentle. Don't blame Lora for her behavior. Focus on what the group needs to do to accomplish its goals.

These examples emphasize two important things about norms. First, don't make norms about unimportant things. Adopting too many norms is like having too many laws in a society. If every aspect of group life is legislated, people feel constrained. They won't feel free to express themselves, which seriously limits input and creativity. Ultimately, this will decrease the chances of group success.

Second, scrutinize norms for their contribution to group effectiveness and productivity. If they don't measure up, eliminate or modify them. Norms are necessary for creating predictable patterns of behavior and similarity in member values and attitudes. They must relate to goals and objectives, however. If norms interfere with achievement and high performance, change them.

Gordon, the leader of the group, has just laid out his plan to increase sales in a specific region. Walter, the sales director in that region, reacts by saying, "You just don't get it, Gordon. What you're proposing won't work in a million years! If you had any sense of the history of this problem or the people in my region, you'd know that. When was the last time you met with us? Was it two or three years ago?"

What You Can Do

This is one of the scarier moments in group life. A member has attacked the leader in a very personal and confrontational way. This kind of confrontation doesn't always happen. In groups that are ultimately successful, disagreements with the leader happen quite a lot. Generally, however, the disagreements are milder, are more tactfully phrased, and don't challenge the leader's competence or intelligence.

Challenging the leader is an essential part of group life. If group members always accept the leader's views, there is no reason to have a group at all. A major reason for working in groups is the assumption that decisions made by groups will be better than those of the best and brightest group member alone. That is, collective intelligence is assumed to be greater than individual intelligence. Although I'm not sure this is always the case, it is the case in a high performance team. The dominance of the leader must be reduced so that others can contribute to that collective intelligence. Disagreements with leaders are necessary at times in order to produce the best decisions and to achieve at high levels.

Obviously, how one disagrees with a leader or another member is key. In the current example, Walter not only disagrees with Gordon's plan but also challenges Gordon personally. He chastises Gordon for his lack of knowledge about the region and for his lack of attention to regional problems. This type of conflict can be very destructive to a group. Some members will be frightened by this situation. Feelings of safety, so essential to group unity, will be undermined, and some members may retreat into silence. Other members may jump to Gordon's defense. Still others may side with Walter in opposition to Gordon. This could lead to a split in the group. It could spell doom for the group if the split cannot be repaired.

You must act quickly to keep these things from happening. Keep a few things in mind as you do this. First, in all likelihood, Gordon is hurt and angry because of what Walter has said. He may also be embarrassed by this public challenge to his leadership and will want to save face. Walter is probably feeling angry, a little embarrassed about his outburst, and anxious about what Gordon will do in response. You should proceed with caution in this emotional situation. You should act, however, because this situation could have very negative effects on the group.

Say something like the following: "I know what it's like to feel loyal to the people back home, Walter. It's hard for any of us to know what's really going on there. All of us, including Gordon, want you to lay out your plans to increase sales. Maybe some others have ideas to contribute, too. Is that okay with everybody?"

Your intention in making this or a similar statement is to refocus the group on developing a plan to increase sales and to defuse the tension between Gordon and Walter. If your intervention works, the focus will return to the task at hand. You will probably get a lot of help from other group members once you say this. Other members will be eager to reduce the mounting tension.

Earlier in this book, I talked about how important it is to avoid getting involved in personality conflicts and personal fights. This example makes clear why this is so important. Nothing threatens group success more than destructive personal arguments.

If you find yourself in a position similar to Walter's, don't do what he did. This situation could have been avoided if Walter had instead said, "I see what your plan is based on, Gordon, but I want to update you on some current issues in the region. Some things have happened that you may not be aware of."

If you find yourself in Gordon's situation someday, and someone like Walter challenges you in a negative way, remember that a leader's job is to work for the good of the group. It would be in the group's best interest for you to say, "You're right, Walter, I may not be aware of some recent developments. Tell me what's been going on lately." This is not easy to do when you're feeling unduly attacked. It's not easy to stifle your urge to retaliate. No one said leadership was easy, however. Do what's best for the group.

Creating a Unified and Effective Group Structure

As Stage 2 groups begin to create an effective group structure, the following things are likely to occur:

- Dissatisfaction with roles surfaces
- Role clarification begins

- Disagreements about strategies to accomplish group tasks surface
- Disagreements about how to make decisions emerge
- Subgroups and coalitions form
- Group intolerance of subgroups, cliques, and coalitions becomes evident
- Increased member participation becomes evident
- Attempts at conflict management begin
- Increased consensus about goals and culture becomes evident near the end of this stage
- Conflict resolution, if successful, increases trust and cohesion

Here is an example of how these issues might occur in a Stage 2 group:

In one of the early meetings, Penny, the group leader, asked you to investigate the budget implications of increasing the sales force in a certain area. At the time, you agreed to do it. After a while, you began to feel uncomfortable with the assignment because you're unfamiliar with the product line in that area. You believe that Jean would do a better job but don't know how to bring this up.

What You Can Do

Perhaps the best way to handle this situation is to approach Penny outside the meeting and say something like this: "I'm feeling a little queasy about my assignment. Jean is more familiar with the product line in that area than I am. She might do a better job. I think she's working on getting the figures for the ad campaign. I'm pretty up on that. Maybe we could switch? If you think it's a good idea, we could suggest a switch at the next meeting."

If the role you are in doesn't match your abilities and talents, try to negotiate for one that does. In the long run, the group will benefit from having the right people in the right roles. Don't avoid challenges, though. Another way to deal with this might be to team up with Jean to work on your assignment. You might learn a lot that way. Whether you switch with or team up with Jean should depend on the group's needs. If time is of the essence, switching is probably best. If developing group members with multiple skills is important to group success, working with Jean on the assignment might be best.

Here's another example:

The group is discussing what to do about a particularly difficult decision it must make. Mary breaks into the conversation and says, "I thought we decided this last week. Doesn't anybody else remember that? This happens all the time. We keep revisiting our decisions. They never seem to stick. No wonder we're behind schedule."

What You Can Do

This is a common situation in groups. Typically, the reason for this is that the group has developed a very informal decision-making process. Sometimes it's so informal that some members don't even know when a decision is being made. There was a time when minutes were taken at every group meeting. There also was a time when votes were taken and members raised their hands to signify their position. Over the years, such practices have been abandoned in favor of more informal meeting procedures. The results of this informality are not always positive. Groups need clear decision-making processes that members accept. How groups make decisions may vary. There is no best decision-making process that should be used in all cases. Regardless of which decision-making process is chosen, however, members and the leader should agree to that process in advance.

In this case, an informal process has been enacted, and I would bet that this was done with no discussion. Like many other aspects of group structure, it just happened without much thought or discussion. You could help in this situation by saying something like, "I remember, Mary, but some other people don't. That worries me. Maybe we should make a list of recent decisions we've made to see what we all remember. It also might be a good idea to talk about how we want to make decisions and whether we should record the decisions we make."

Let's look at this example:

In an effort to get tasks done faster, group members have decided to delegate some tasks to a subgroup of three members. These three are to report back to the group when they have finished. Lately, however, some other members have become a little irritated with and suspicious of members of the subgroup. They wonder what they're doing and seem to feel excluded by them. They even seem to resent the fact that "The Group of Three" tend to talk with each other more than with the rest of the members.

What You Can Do

Establishing subgroups is a logical way to increase group output and task performance. Division of labor is necessary whenever complex tasks must be completed in a timely manner. Logical though it may be, it is usually perceived by others as a threat to group unity and cohesion. This is a normal human response. Remember how it felt in high school when you weren't invited to join a popular clique? Even if you didn't really want to be part of that group, it didn't feel good to be excluded. We may be all grown up, but some of those feelings remain. Most people want to be in on things. We want to know what others are doing. We want to belong.

In a Stage 2 group, trust is just beginning to build. Members haven't developed enough faith in the trustworthiness of their colleagues to be certain that a subset of them will work for the good of the whole group. Maybe they're looking out for themselves or talking about other members in their private meetings. Although this may sound paranoid, human beings do have a bit of a paranoid streak.

There are two options in situations like this. The group could choose not to use subgroups to accomplish tasks, or members could use the emergence of subgroups as an opportunity to increase group trust and cohesion. Obviously, I endorse the latter. The emergence of subgroups is very important to group effectiveness. It's a sign that the group is getting organized, and an organized group is much more likely to be successful. Learning to tolerate and to trust subgroups, then, is vital to group success.

If you're not a member of the subgroup and you've noticed that other nonmembers (perhaps yourself included) are uncomfortable with subgroup members, you might say something like the following: "We're not very comfortable yet with delegating tasks to subgroups. Maybe it would help if the subgroups we created reported more frequently about what they're working on. That might help them stay on track and help the rest of us feel more comfortable. It would also give the subgroup members the opportunity to get some input from us and give us some ideas as well."

If you are a member of the subgroup and you've noticed that others seem a little uncomfortable with you, you could raise the same issue by saying, "The three of us have been thinking that we'd like to keep you up to date about what we're doing. Could we get five minutes on the agenda to fill you in and ask for advice if we need it?"

Box 8.1   Holy War

An interfaith group of priests, nuns, and ministers was in conflict. The male priests and ministers blamed the nuns for the group's problem. They accused the nuns of being too enamored of discussion and dialogue. The men felt that all this talk was going nowhere. After I worked with this group for a while, it became clear that the real problem was that the group didn't have a clear decision-making procedure. Once a decision-making procedure was in place, peace was restored.

Also, if you're a member of a subgroup, keep your commitments. If you are scheduled to report back to the whole group on a given date, do so. This is always important to do, especially for the first few subgroups. If early subgroups keep other members and leaders informed of their progress and keep their commitments, group trust and cohesion will increase significantly.

Here's one last example:

Marie and Tim are arguing about the best way to raise money for the new wing of the museum. Grants and state funding will provide 60% of what's needed. The museum staff must raise the rest. Marie believes her plan will raise the most money in the shortest time, and Tim believes his plan will raise the most money in the shortest time. The rest of the staff have taken sides, and the disagreement is intense.

What You Can Do

Conflict resolution is an essential component of group success. If this becomes a long, drawn-out disagreement, nobody benefits. You can help in this situation by saying something like this: "Let's stop for a minute and outline both plans in detail. Then we can see what we're really talking about in terms of investment of money and staff time. Who knows? Maybe there's a way to combine aspects of both plans. We won't know that, though, until we go over each plan in detail. What do the rest of you think?"

The second stage of group development can be difficult. The goals of this stage are not easy. On U.S. coins is the phrase *e pluribus unum*, which means "from many, one." From many individuals with many points of view, one group must be forged with a coherent culture and structure that will facilitate goal achievement. This is no easy task, but it is made less difficult if members know what to expect and how to help each other accomplish it.

⚜ NINE ⚜

REORGANIZING AT STAGE 3

―――――◆●◆――――――

Goals of Stage 3

If a group manages to work through the inevitable conflicts of Stage 2, then members' trust, commitment to the group, and willingness to cooperate increase. Communication becomes more open and task oriented. Members focus more on the task and less on issues of status, power, or influence. This third stage of group development, called the trust and structure phase, is characterized by more mature negotiations about roles, organization, and procedures. It is also a time in which members work to solidify positive relationships with each other.

Some things that happen during Stage 3 are described next.

Fine-Tuning Roles, Organization, and Procedures

In the process of fine-tuning roles, the level of organization, and group procedures, the following things are likely to occur:

- Goal clarity and consensus about goals increase
- Roles and tasks are adjusted to increase the likelihood of goal achievement
- The leader's role becomes less directive and more consultative
- The communication structure becomes more flexible
- The content of communication becomes more task oriented

- Tolerance of subgroups, cliques, and coalitions increases
- Greater division of labor occurs
- Conflict continues to occur, but it is managed more effectively

Here is an example of how these issues might occur in a Stage 3 group:

Phyllis, the group's leader, is actively engaged in the group's discussion. A member named John is running the meeting. Phyllis brings up some new ideas, but after some discussion the group decides to go with another plan. Then the group runs into a snag. Members are unsure how to implement the plan. Everyone turns to Phyllis for her input.

What You Can Do

At the third stage of group development, leaders are not as prominent as they were in earlier stages. By this time, members are beginning to take over some leadership functions. In this example, a member is running the meeting, which allows the leader to participate more actively in the discussion. Members are much more comfortable with and, in general, less dependent on the leader for direction. This way of operating is new for the group, however, and there will be moments when the group may revert to previous ways of behaving. In this case, when the group could not reach a decision, members looked to the leader for direction.

This situation is quite common. Development doesn't proceed in one direction. We often take two steps forward and one step back. On the one hand, members and the leader should be mindful of this tendency but not overly concerned. On the other hand, members and leaders should strive to support forward motion. If Phyllis makes this decision for the group, it won't be the end of the world, but it may slow progress a bit.

If you are a member of the group, you could help by saying something like, "Hey, let's try to resolve this issue as a group. There's no need to put this on Phyllis. We've dealt with tougher issues than this before." Obviously, you should make this statement with good humor and a smile.

If you are Phyllis, you may feel the urge to "save the group" by making the decision. Try to resist that urge. It would probably be best to say something like, "Let's discuss this a while longer and see what we come up with."

Here's another situation that might arise in a Stage 3 group:

Todd just came back from a fishing trip. He is telling fish stories that are pretty funny. Everyone is enjoying listening to him. He's been talking for about five minutes, and the meeting is scheduled to last an hour. A number of issues must be dealt with in that hour.

What You Can Do

Having a bit of fun at a meeting is a positive thing and a sign that people are comfortable with each other. It reduces stress and can increase feelings of cohesion. When the fun goes on too long, however, productivity may be compromised. In a Stage 3 group, members are very interested in work. Their conversations are more task oriented, and everyone is interested in being efficient and productive. The group is not a high performance team yet, but members want the group to reach high levels of productivity.

There is nothing inherently wrong with Todd's fish stories. However, if you are beginning to worry about getting work done, or if you sense that others are, you might say, "Todd, these stories are wonderful, but it's time for us to get to work."

Annette has just returned from a meeting with Nancy, the vice president, and other project leaders. She reports the details of the meeting to the group members. She's a little worried because two coordinating groups are being set up to oversee aspects of the overall contract. Annette feels stretched to the max and says, "I don't know how I can attend all these meetings, get my other work done, and be responsible to the group."

What You Can Do

One of the hallmarks of a Stage 3 group is that members begin to take on aspects of the leadership role. One important aspect of that role is to communicate and negotiate with other parts of the organization. Groups can lose their way if members don't maintain open communication with other groups that are relevant to their success.

In today's workplace, everyone is busy. Most people I run into feel overloaded. Interacting with other relevant groups is important to group success, however. You could help by saying something like, "Annette, maybe a few of us could represent our group at those meetings. Someone needs to go, but I don't think it has to be you."

Solidifying Positive Relationships

In the process of building positive relationships among group members, the following things are likely to occur:

- Cohesion and trust increase
- Member satisfaction increases
- Cooperation becomes more evident
- Individual commitment to group goals and tasks is high
- Voluntary conformity with group norms increases
- Helpful deviation is tolerated

Examples of how these things might occur in Stage 3 groups are provided next.

Al is an odd duck. He doesn't say much during meetings and seems to spend his time doodling on a notepad. For the first few months, group members were uncomfortable with Al and rarely asked for his opinion. After all, he didn't seem to care enough to participate. Every once in a while, though, Al would say something that was right on and very helpful. When it comes to engine design, he really knows his stuff.

What You Can Do

This group has developed a strong norm for participation, and that is a very good thing. It's difficult to develop a high performance team without the participation of the majority of members. For whatever reasons, Al is not a talker. This makes others uncomfortable with him, and they question his commitment to the group. They don't perceive him as a team player. On the other hand, when Al does say something, it's worth listening to him. What he does say is usually very helpful.

Ignoring Al or insisting that he become a more active participant will not help the situation. Al is Al, after all. You could help by noticing the kinds of input that Al contributes and, when those topics come up, asking Al for his

> ### Box 9.1   Strangest Goal
>
> I asked a team what their goal was, and they said, in unison, "To be a cohesive team." I asked them whether the company paid them well for their efforts.

thoughts. You could say, "Al knows more about this than any of us. Can you help us out with this, Al?"

People are different. Some of us are talkers and some of us are not. Some of us follow rules and norms to the letter. Some of us don't. As long as people are making a positive contribution to the group, however small, let them be. The workplace values conformity, and some degree of conformity is necessary if groups are to be successful, but too much conformity can be a negative. If we are all behaving and thinking in the same way, generating new ideas may be difficult. Sometimes, oddball ideas are the best ideas.

Some people in the group are expressing concern about whether Colleen, Barbara, and Chris will finish their report in time. They didn't come to the meeting today, and no one knows why.

What You Can Do

By the third stage of group development, trust is pretty high. However, there will be moments when feelings of mistrust surface. This is natural, especially when time is of the essence. Most readers probably know people like Colleen, Barbara, and Chris. They're just worried about staying on schedule.

You could help by saying something like, "Colleen, Barbara, and Chris will get it done. They're as worried about deadlines as we are. They may need some help, though. I'd be willing to check in with them this week and offer a hand if they need it."

Brigid has been asked by the group to fill in the details of a new insurance product that members are considering. She's been working on this project for two weeks. At the meeting, Brigid says, "I've got most of the details worked out, but a few things have me stumped. I could use some help."

What You Can Do

In the competitive world of business, asking for help isn't easy. The fact that Brigid asked for help is a sign that she trusts other group members and that she is committed to doing the best possible job. This is terrific and should be encouraged.

You could help by saying something like, "Can you tell us what's got you stumped? I'm sure one of us could help. If not, someone probably knows who to go to for the answers."

The third stage of group development is a time when group processes and procedures are adjusted so that the group can work at higher levels of performance. Some issues were already resolved at Stage 2, but other norms, strategies, and roles must be scrutinized to ensure that they contribute to group achievement.

Now that group members have resolved many earlier issues, trust has increased. Members feel comfortable enough to question how the group is functioning and to suggest changes to increase the chances of success. It's a time to get more organized and to plan better ways of working together. It's also the time to solidify working relationships among members.

One word of caution is necessary here. Some groups enter Stage 3 and focus too much energy on building relationships and not enough on getting organized. These groups begin to resemble love-ins after a while. Members are so busy supporting each other that they forget to make sure that the way they're working together is the best way. Remember that research suggests that members should spend about 15% to 20% of group time focusing on supporting each other. The rest should be focused as much as possible on work. Often, groups focus too much energy on getting organized and forget to support and encourage each other in that endeavor. This is a classic formula for burnout. If members don't feel supported by the group and others external to the group, they will become disillusioned and resentful. If that happens, the group will find itself back at Stage 2 in a flash.

TEN

SUSTAINING HIGH PERFORMANCE

Goals of Stage 4

As its name implies, the fourth, or work, stage of group development is a time of intense productivity and effectiveness. It is at this stage that a work group becomes a team. Having resolved most of the issues of the previous stages, the team can focus most of its energy on goal achievement and task accomplishment. Although work occurs at every developmental stage, the quality and quantity of work increase significantly during Stage 4.

The goals of Stage 4 include getting the work done well, making decisions, remaining cohesive while encouraging task-related conflicts, and maintaining high performance over the long haul.

Sadly, many people have never been members of a Stage 4 team. They don't know what it's like to work at high performance levels and to enjoy the experience. Some teams that make it to Stage 4 contain members for whom this is a new experience. They are excited by the ease with which work gets done. They are thrilled with the feelings of camaraderie and trust generated by the team. They are happy they are learning so much and are eager for this experience to continue for as long as possible. The problem is that unless members are careful, backsliding may occur.

Getting to Stage 4 is not easy. Many groups never do. Staying at Stage 4 isn't easy, either. Without constant vigilance, teams may regress to earlier stages of development. To maintain high levels of performance for an extended

---

Box 10.1   Pride Cometh . . .

Two groups were working on similar projects. They asked for feedback on how they were doing. I assessed both groups and gave them suggestions on how to improve. The Stage 3 group used the feedback and worked hard to improve. The Stage 4 team didn't. They felt they were doing great and would beat the other group easily. They did not.

---

period of time, team members need to learn some things and to do some things that will keep their effectiveness and performance at high levels. Some of the things that high performance teams do to remain effective are described next.

Getting the Work Done Well

The norms in high performance teams support not only getting the work done but also getting the work done well. Those norms include the following:

- Team norms encourage high performance and quality
- The team expects to be successful
- The team encourages innovation
- The team pays attention to the details of its work

Here is an example of how these norms are enacted in high performance teams:

Felice has just suggested a way to get things done faster by eliminating a few steps where quality checks are made. After all, there are other points in the process where the quality is checked. She believes this will save valuable time and some money as well. You aren't sure this is a good idea.

What You Can Do

One of the goals of a Stage 4 team is to get the work done well. Norms for quality and high performance have been established, and everyone wants to do the best job possible. You know that Felice does as well. She also wants to save time and money, which isn't a bad idea if it can be done without compromising quality. Felice's idea will save money. There's no doubt of that. You're not sure how her plan will affect product quality, however.

Given that the goal is to get the work done well, you might say something like, "Felice, I think we should go over your plan very carefully. I'm as eager as you are to save money and time. I just want to make sure that product quality won't be affected."

The point of saying this is to remind everyone of the norm for quality as well as for high performance. As work intensifies and deadlines loom, it's easy to forget commitments to quality. Gentle reminders are very helpful.

Felice agrees with you that quality is important and describes her plan in more detail. She says there are enough checks at other points in the process to ensure that quality is not compromised. You and other team members are impressed with Felice's careful evaluation of the steps in the process. She really did her homework.

What You Can Do

Part of getting the job done well is to encourage team members to be innovative. Felice has come up with an innovative idea, and, after lengthy team discussion, members think her idea is a good one. You might say, "Felice, I didn't understand at first, but you've made a believer out of me. I say we go with your idea. What do the rest of you think?"

Here's another example:

Renaya is feeling overwhelmed by the team's current workload. She says, "I'm not sure we can do all this by the end of the month. It seems like too much for us to handle."

What You Can Do

Even members of Stage 4 teams can become anxious about team success. Teams can also set goals for themselves that are too ambitious. The feeling that the team will succeed is vital to high performance. If teams become uncertain about goal achievement, there will be negative repercussions. You want the team to maintain its expectation of success. You also want to address Renaya's concern. You might say, "Renaya, I think we should review our plans for the month. Maybe they are too ambitious. Maybe we haven't divided the workload evenly enough. It could be that you got more than your share. What do the rest of you think about this?"

The team is planning a meeting with the production team to establish the time frame for launching a new product. Dan has been given the responsibility for working out the agenda with George, who heads the production team. Dan has just presented the agenda to the group. Jane says, "Dan, I think that the agenda includes most of what we need to clear up, but I'm a little concerned about coordinating marketing and production timelines. Shouldn't marketing be included in that meeting?"

What You Can Do

Because paying attention to details is an important component of group success, you might say something like this: "I agree with Jane, Dan. Marketing should be represented at the meeting. I also think it would be a good idea to go over the agenda again to make doubly sure we've covered everything and have all the right players at the meeting." If you are Dan, don't get defensive. People aren't trying to find fault with your work. In Stage 4 teams, everyone is committed to getting the work done well. Reviewing plans and checking things twice are expressions of that commitment.

Making Decisions

Decision making in high performance teams is a careful process that involves the following:

- The team spends time defining problems it must solve or decisions it must make
- The team spends time planning how it will solve problems and make decisions
- The team spends enough time discussing problems that must be solved and decisions that must be made
- The team uses participatory methods for decision making
- The team implements and evaluates its solutions and decisions

Following is an example of how a high performance team makes decisions and what you can do to help.

Kate says, "Can't we just change the schedule of the show so that it doesn't occur on the same weekend as the Motherwell exhibit at the museum? I don't want our artist to be overshadowed by anything." Mike says, "I agree with you, but I'm worried about what that will do to the whole schedule."

What You Can Do

The team is about to make a decision. You know that in order to make a good decision, the team needs to define the problem clearly. It may seem that the problem is clear: Another institution has scheduled an exhibit that may keep people from attending your institution's art exhibit. Before rearranging your schedule, however, it would make sense to make sure you have defined the problem correctly. You might say, "You might be right that the Motherwell show will compete with ours. I'd feel better, though, if we talked about that a little before we start thinking of solutions."

Lise has a different take on the situation. She thinks that the Motherwell show will attract different people. Midge disagrees. She says, "Motherwell has earned a place in art history. Even people who are not particularly attracted to his work will go to the exhibit because of his stature in contemporary art." Other group members begin to take sides with either Lise or Midge.

What You Can Do

Defining problems clearly often entails going beyond the team for information. You might say, "I think we're stuck. We have two different opinions about this. Maybe we should ask some other people for their thoughts on this. Who might know more about this kind of situation than we do?"

Lise and Midge contact three curators whose institutions had exhibits that were held at the same time as exhibits of well-known figures in the art world. All three said that attendance at their exhibits was higher than expected. People who came from out of town for the major exhibit made the rounds of other art exhibits and shows in the area. Kate remains unconvinced.

What You Can Do

You might say, "Kate, I think the team is ready to make a decision on this. We usually vote and go with the majority. Since this is really important to you, I think it would be best in this case to try to reach consensus on this decision. Let's discuss all the options again and see if we can come up with a decision that everyone can live with. Is that okay with everybody?"

By suggesting a change in the decision-making process, you are making it clear to everyone that Kate's position has to be taken seriously. You are also reminding Kate that the team cares about her and also must take action on this issue. In this team, consensus does not mean that everyone has to be enthusiastic about a decision. It simply means that everyone can live with the decision. After further discussion, Kate may still be skeptical, but she may be willing to go along with the emerging consensus. She may agree to go along this time as an experiment. It is unlikely that Kate will attempt to block the decision. This team has established a norm that encourages members to go along with decisions as long as the team has done its best to discuss the problem, to uncover relevant information, and to seek input from all members.

Cohesion and Conflict

Positive relationships are evident in high performance teams. Conflicts continue to occur as well. In high performance teams, the following characteristics are in evidence:

- The team is highly cohesive
- Interpersonal attraction among members is high
- Members are cooperative
- Periods of conflict are frequent but brief
- The team has effective conflict management strategies

Here is an example of how teams remain cohesive and deal with conflict:

The team has been thrown a curveball. The court date has been moved up because of political pressure, and this legal defense team must be prepared for trial much earlier than expected. Members of the team know there's no chance of getting the date moved back. They'll just have to be ready.

What You Can Do

You might say something like, "I was planning to go away for the weekend, but I'll cancel that. That will give me time to work with Janice on preparing those motions. What do you say, Janice?"

Teams, at Stage 4, step up to challenges. The world is not predictable. What's more, it is often stressful. In teams that are functioning well, people make the necessary adjustments to get the job done. A word of caution is in order here. If members find themselves in situations like this frequently, it may be a sign that they should review their operational procedures. Too many situations like this one may overload team members and cause burnout. This particular situation seems unavoidable. Others may be avoidable with some forethought, however.

Here's another example:

Bob is getting hot under the collar. He strongly disagrees with Tom's proposed changes in patient education procedures for the unit. "Sure, these changes will save time, but I will not compromise patient care for anybody." Tom is hurt by this statement and says, "I'm not trying to do that. I'm just trying to standardize our approach to patient education. That is what will save the time."

What You Can Do

You know that conflicts occur at every stage of group development. In fact, conflicts are good because they help provide clarity. You also know that the way conflicts are handled is critical. So you say, "This is a very important issue. I think we should take both these points of view very seriously and get other members' opinions as well. In fact, it might be useful to see what other units like ours are doing about patient education. What do the rest of you think?"

As the conversation is redirected away from Bob and Tom and back to the team as a whole, tempers will undoubtedly cool. Both men's concerns have been acknowledged and taken seriously. Other members will have the opportunity to weigh in on these issues, and the idea of seeking information from other hospitals will probably be received positively by team members. The trick in conflict situations is to intervene quickly and stay focused on the task.

Maintaining High Performance

High performance is maintained in Stage 4 in the following ways:

- The team gets, gives, and uses feedback about its effectiveness and productivity
- The team evaluates its performance on a regular basis
- The team takes steps to avoid routine and getting stuck in a rut

Examples of how teams maintain high performance and what you can do to help are provided next.

John is facilitating this meeting. The team rotates the job of meeting facilitator, which gives Joyce, the designated leader, the chance to participate more fully in discussions. Halfway through the meeting, John says, "It's time to do a process check."

What You Can Do

This is a simple one. Because you know it's important to evaluate team processes regularly, go along with John's suggestion. There are three ways to evaluate how a team is doing. The first way, which John has suggested, is to take five minutes in the middle of a meeting to answer the following questions:

- Are we on task and on schedule in terms of covering the agenda?
- Does everyone think that she or he has been heard?
- Does anything need clarification at this point?
- Is there anything we could do at this point to improve our process?

Taking the time to do a quick evaluation halfway through the meeting is called a process check. Process checks make it possible to correct things that are not going well during the meeting so that changes can be made right away. This prevents the team from spending time unproductively.

Bill, the group leader, says, "At the next meeting, we're scheduled to do a periodic review of how the team is doing. Take the next few minutes to fill out the checklist. Patrick has volunteered to summarize the results for us and to present the summary at the next meeting."

What You Can Do

This one is easy, too. Go along with Bill's suggestion. Respond to the checklist as honestly as possible. The second way to ensure continual evaluation is to do periodic reviews of team function as Bill has suggested. The length of time between reviews will vary for each team. In general, once every six to eight weeks seems reasonable. The idea is to avoid long periods of lowered productivity by making any necessary changes as soon as possible.

In Chapter 4, I introduced the Team Performance Checklist. Every six to eight weeks, all members and the leader should take a few minutes at the end of a meeting to complete the checklist. One member should be asked to organize the responses and present the results at the next meeting. The best way to organize the responses is to determine the average response to each question and the average total response.

Begin the next meeting by going over the responses. Look at items where the average response is high (3 or 4). These are things that the team is doing well. Keep doing those things. Next, look at items where the average response is low (1 or 2). Discuss strategies to improve the team's performance in those areas. Implement those strategies immediately. Don't forget to check up on yourselves. Do another evaluation about two months later. Repeat the process just described and make any necessary changes.

To some readers, this may seem like a waste of time. It's not. The dynamics of groups and teams can shift quickly. Before you know it, regression to earlier stages can occur. Teams do not operate in a vacuum. Changes in the external environment can take their toll on the best teams. Budget cuts, downsizing, shifts in organizational priorities, and many other things can affect internal team functioning. Stage 4 teams are not immune to these things. They do have a better chance of surviving these pressures than groups at lower developmental levels, but only if they are vigilant.

Internal forces can also affect team dynamics. Work pressures, new members, conflicts that arise, and lots of other things can turn a silk purse into a sow's ear. Getting to the top of the development ladder is hard. Staying there is just as hard.

Oscar is worried that the team isn't getting enough feedback about its performance from others outside the team. He says, "I think we should try to figure out ways to get better and more regular feedback from others in the organization. We get so caught up in doing the work that we don't take the time to find out what others think of the quality of that work. Can we make that an agenda item at our next meeting?"

What You Can Do

Support Oscar's effort to get the team to discuss ways to get feedback. The third way to evaluate team effectiveness and productivity requires feedback from sources outside the team. Some teams get constant feedback about their performance. Others get almost none. All teams need to figure out ways to determine whether they are meeting goals and whether others are satisfied with their progress and output. Without feedback, it's impossible to know how to improve.

The type of feedback and methods to get that feedback will vary from team to team. The ease or difficulty of devising methods to obtain that feedback will as well. If the team's goals are concrete, getting feedback will be easier. If goals are more abstract, it will be harder. For example, if the goal of the team is to increase the number of cars produced in a quarter, feedback is easy to obtain. On the other hand, if the task of the team is to improve the corporate climate, obtaining timely feedback will be more difficult. Whether it is difficult or hard to obtain, without feedback the team is flying blind. Figure out ways to obtain performance feedback on a regular basis.

By the way, although I included these evaluation strategies in a discussion of Stage 4 teams, assessing group progress and obtaining performance feedback are necessary at every stage of development. Do it early and often throughout the life of your group.

Jane says, "I've been feeling a little flat at meetings for the past month. Are we getting a little dull? We were such pistols for quite a while, but I think we're starting to bore each other a little. Is there something we can do to spice things up?"

What You Can Do

My colleagues and I have been doing research on work teams for years. One of the things we've noticed is that teams tend to experience process losses as they age. We've noticed that after about 18 to 24 months, teams that were working at high levels start to falter. Productivity and effectiveness begin to decrease. No one is sure why this happens, but I think it may be the result of fatigue. Team members simply get tired of doing the same old things in the same old way even when those things have been effective. After all the work that goes into creating a high performance team, members tire of it. They want something new and different.

This is not surprising. Human beings tend to be a bit perverse in this regard. After spending years renovating a house, its occupants tire of the décor. After years of living somewhere, some people feel the urge to move. After months of eating a salad for lunch every day, the thought of another salad bores us to tears. We long for stability, and when we achieve it we want something different and challenging.

Teams are composed of humans, and so the urge for novelty and change influences team members. When things become too routine, most of us want change. Our attention goes to other things and away from maintaining high levels of performance.

Again, this is as natural as can be, but from a work perspective it may have negative consequences. If the work of the team is completed, it might be best to disband and to distribute the now-routine tasks to others. If the work is not complete, however, team members will need to think of ways to revitalize themselves. Some ways to do this follow:

- Add new goals and interesting tasks for the team to work on
- Hold a retreat focused on ways to revitalize team members
- Switch roles around so that members are doing new and different things
- Teach each other new aspects of the work
- Rotate some members off the team and add new members
- Change the way meetings are conducted
- Change the meeting time
- Do other creative things to energize the process

Stage 4 is the best of times. Do whatever it takes to ensure that "the best of times" doesn't become "the good old days."

ELEVEN

VIRTUAL TEAMS

O ver the years, nine of my colleagues and I have trained and certified 1,159 people to become GDQ consultants. Most of these GDQ consultants work with face-to-face groups. At the present time, 754 consultants have used the paper version of the Group Development Questionnaire to determine what stage a work group is in and to plan what they can to do to help work group members and their leader improve their performance and create a more effective work team.

Four hundred and six consultants have worked with virtual teams for the same reasons. Virtual teams are groups whose members and leaders don't work together face to face very often or at all. Unlike traditional team members and their leader, who work together in a room, virtual team members and their leader may be in different parts of their organization, in different states, or in different countries. Of course, members or leaders might be sending e-mails from their homes, airports or coffee shops as well. For example, I go to work in Europe two or three times a year. I will be sending e-mails from Europe and my team in the United States will be responding. This is referred to as computer-mediated discourse. In a very real way, computer-mediated discourse has changed the world of work.

Researchers Ale Ebrahim, Ahmed, and Taha (2009) describe a virtual team as a "geographically dispersed team, distributed team, or remote team in which individual members work together across time, space, and organizational boundaries, with links strengthened by webs of communication technology" (p. 2667). Powell, Piccoli, and Ives (2004) define virtual teams as "groups of geographically, organizationally and/or time dispersed works brought together by information and telecommunication technologies to accomplish one or more organizational tasks" (p. 7). A body of research on virtual teams has developed over the last decade that supports the utility, and necessity, of virtual teams. The number of face-to-face teams is becoming smaller and the number of virtual teams working in business, health care, education, manufacturing, and other enterprises is increasing. Even high school and university project teams work together virtually more than face to face.

A recent Society for Human Resource Management (www.shrm.com) survey of 379 human resource professionals found that 46% of organizations use virtual teams for communication. Organizations with multinational operations use virtual teams 66% of the time, which makes a great deal of sense. In U.S. organizations, however, only 28% of work teams use virtual teams. In the near future, that will change.

Fifty-three percent of human resource professionals say that virtual teams are necessary because of increased interaction among organizations. Organizations with multinational operations employ virtual teams 66% of the time. However, U.S. government agencies use virtual teams only 9% of the time. Fifty percent of for-profit companies use virtual teams, and privately owned for-profit companies employ virtual teams about 46% of the time.

The majority of human resource professionals working in organizations believe that virtual teams are necessary to increase interaction among international organizations. Another interesting finding is that 39% of organizations use virtual teams to increase productivity and another 39% use virtual teams to minimize cost.

In the next few sections of this chapter, I will describe four virtual venues that are often used to support and assist work team members and leaders. These are video conferences, LinkedIn, Skype, and blogs.

Video Conferences

When I was teaching master's and doctoral graduate students at Temple University, I was introduced to video conferencing. Like many universities at that time, Temple had two locations. One location was in Philadelphia and the other was in Harrisburg. For some time, I had to drive 180 miles round trip between the two locations. This was not fun.

Fortunately, the university installed video conferencing in both locations at about that time, which made my work much easier. Video conferencing allowed my student work teams in one location to communicate with each other and with me. In this case, multipoint video conferencing allowed student work team members in one location to sit in a room and communicate with team members in another location. Many researchers believe that video conferencing continues to remain the fastest-growing segment of the computer industry.

LinkedIn

GDQ consultants often ask other consultants for help with a difficult work group. However, instead of sending an e-mail to a single colleague, GDQ consultants in Europe and the United States have established their own LinkedIn online network. They can ask for help with a difficult work group, or suggest strategies for helping a work group to improve their performance and become a high performance team. From all reports, this has been a very useful process. Without a doubt, LinkedIn is very useful to GDQ consultants.

Skype

Skype provides verbal voice, video, screen sharing, instant messaging, and direct file transfers. Skype is also capable of making international phone calls. Over 40 million individuals across the world use Skype. Skype has been used by GDQ consultants across the world.

Here is an example of Skype's usefulness: A virtual team contained a group of research scientists from different countries. The researchers' goal was to increase the quantity and quality of food in countries where food was very scarce. Planning ways to accomplish this goal required discussion among the researchers. They wanted to discuss alternative methods of achieving these goals. An earlier form of Skype was their method of choice.

Also, the researchers wanted to see how well they were working together and what they could do to become a high performance team. In conjunction with GDQ consultants, the researchers employed the strategies described in this book. At first, the research team was in Stage 1. The GDQ consultants worked with them to improve their performance. After a few months, the research team was functioning as a high performance team. As a result, the quantity of food in selected areas increased significantly over time.

Over the years, I have trained individual consultants to assess work groups and help group members and leaders to improve their performance. At this point, approximately 857 work groups in the U.S. have worked to improve group performance. In Europe, about 642 have done the same.

Blogging

A blog is one type of virtual grouping. It is a site for discussion and information sharing on a particular topic. Blogs are connected to the World Wide Web. In blogs, individuals ask questions, discuss a specific topic, and share information about that topic. Blogging is done in a virtual online sight.

However, bloggers are not work teams. Rather, bloggers are individuals interested in discussing a chosen topic, or question, with other individuals. Some blogs involve a small number of individual participants. Others involve hundreds, if not thousands, of people. Blogs do not directly relate to virtual teams that are goal directed and focused on improving work team development. However, team members and team consultants often explore blogs to seek out information related to their work groups.

Virtual GDQ Online Scoring Systems

A number of years ago, when I was working with an organization in Michigan, I was in an airport waiting to board a plane. I had my computer on my shoulder. A man in a hurry ran into me, and my computer dropped to the floor. It was severely damaged. Fortunately, when I arrived at my destination, I had enough copies of the paper version of the GDQ questionnaire to gather the results by hand. But that wasn't much fun either.

Based on that experience, two virtual scoring systems were developed. One was the GDQ Online Scoring System. This online program has been on my website for some time now, and certified GDQ consultants can access the GDQ website and to use the program at any time.

The Learning Bridge is a company that develops all kinds of questionnaires. With the help of Learning Bridge staff, another virtual GDQ scoring system was developed.

Certified GDQ consultants can access either of the GDQ scoring systems.

Star Trek Changed the World

When I was a doctoral student at the University of Wisconsin, I analyzed my research data on a computer that was about 20 feet long and 7 feet high. To organize my data, I needed lots of punch cards. Each punch card consisted of different patterns of zeros and ones. Somehow those zeros and ones generated an analysis of statistical data and the research results that were incorporated into my dissertation.

The process was tedious and took forever.

Star Trek movies and television shows taught us about virtual team work and collaboration. Also, Star Trek showed us a number of imagined technologies that we eventually adopted and developed in the real world. Cell phones, much better computers, data analysis methods, conferencing, Skype, virtual teams, and the like led research scientists to learn about, and create, new products and methods that we use today.

❄ TWELVE ❄

RECENT RESEARCH

———◦❖◦———

Since this is the final chapter of the fifth edition of *Creating Effective Teams*, I want to answer the questions that work group members and leaders have asked. I will do my best to do that.

On Average, How Long Does the Development Process Take?

Although team members and the leader are eager to reach Stage 4, it takes time for that to happen. Based on the results of a number of research analyses, Table 12.1 describes how groups move through the stages. It is important for work groups members and the leader to understand this and to move through the process in an orderly manner. As I said earlier, work to accomplish each stage and then move to the next stage.

Table 12.1   How Long the Team Development Process Takes, in Months

Stage 1	Dependency and Inclusion	2.6
Stage 2	Counterdependency and Fighting	3.7
Stage 3	Trust and Structure	4.7
Stage 4	Work and Productivity	4.7–8.5

Does Group Size Affect Group Productivity?

Group size is an important factor for group development and group productivity. The good news is that group leaders and members prefer small groups about 80% of the time. Based on the data previously described, group members and leaders choose small groups, as opposed to larger groups, for a number of reasons. Smaller groups function better than larger groups. In small groups, each individual member and the leader can discuss her or his ideas and participate in decision making. In larger groups, a number of members may not have the opportunity to speak; usually, a small number of members discuss things while the rest of the members listen. This process excludes some members' thoughts and ideas as a result.

Table 12.2 Group Members and Leaders' Preferred Group Size (N = 709)

3–7 participants = 327	46%
8–12 participants = 243	34%
13–17 participants = 56	8%
18+ participants = 83	12%

If decisions must be agreed on by a large group, there is a strategy that can be very useful to that large work group. For example, I was asked to help a teacher group that monitored elementary educational progress in the state of Massachusetts. This group contained 40 professionals, and the group met once a week. When I arrived, I was directed to the room the group was working in. All 40 members, including the leader, were sitting around the largest table I'd ever seen. The table barely fit in the room.

I observed their discussion for a while, but it was hard to hear what people were saying. Members were having problems hearing as well. I suggested that members break into groups of five, and that each subgroup discuss a particular issue. This worked well. Each small group reported their ideas to the large group and received input from their colleagues. That process was very successful and has been continued to this day.

Does Group Age in Months Affect Group Productivity?

Based on the data I have collected, the age of work groups does influence productivity. The older groups become, the less productive they become. Members and leaders in younger groups function better and are generally more productive than older groups. As a result, it would be helpful to limit the length of time that a group spends working. Of course, this is not always possible. Some groups, such as faculty groups and management groups, go on forever, with a member occasionally leaving and others joining the ongoing group. The implication of this finding is that planning ahead is important. Often, group members and their leader assume that a team can function at a high level in a very short period of time. As you know, this is not the case.

Table 12.3   Productivity of Work Groups According to Group Age
(N = 521)

1–5 months (n = 108)	**21%**
6–10 months (n = 151)	**29%**
11–15 months (n = 116)	**22%**
16–20 months (n = 83)	**16%**
21–25 months (n = 63)	**12%**

How Do Work Groups in Different Sectors Function?

Currently there are 815 work groups in my database, including those involved in business, manufacturing, education, and health care. I was curious to know whether the performance of work groups in these sectors was similar or different.

Business work group members at Stage 1 spent 27% of their time listening to their manager's goals and responding with questions for the manager. This is normal. However, if this pattern continues for some time and members continued to take direction from their manager, creativity, suggestions from members, and discussions between members and the leader will be limited at best. I have observed many business work groups whose leader defines goals, and assign roles, to different members while members take dictation.

Table 12.4 Business Work Groups at the Various Stage of Development (N = 416)

STAGE 1 n = 113	27%	STAGE 2 n = 82	20%
STAGE 3 n = 128	30%	STAGE 4 n = 93	23%

Business work groups in Stage 2 spent less time challenging the manager's ideas and clarifying goals in comparison to work groups in the other stages. Only 20% of the work groups were in Stage 2, which means that goals were often not clear.

Members and leaders of Stage 3 groups spent time organizing to become high performance teams and developing solid relationships among team members. However, only 23% of work groups functioned well enough to be considered high performance teams.

Table 12.5 Manufacturing Work Groups at the Various Stage of Development (N = 175)

STAGE 1 n = 39	23%	STAGE 2 n = 43	24%
STAGE 3 n = 55	31%	STAGE 4 n = 38	22%

At Stage 3, manufacturing work groups spent most of their time organizing and preparing to become high performance teams. Some of those work groups did become high performance teams. However, reaching that level, and remaining at that level, is difficult. Only 22% of manufacturing teams became high performance teams.

Teachers work most of their time alone in the classroom. However, teachers and the principal meet together as faculty groups to discuss educational goals for their students and ways to improve student performance. Discussions about these goals occur at Stage 2. Based on the data outlined

Table 12.6   Education Work Groups at the Various Stage of Development
(N = 128)

STAGE 1 n = 28	21%	STAGE 2 n = 20	16%
STAGE 3 n = 48	38%	STAGE 4 n = 32	25%

in Table 12.6, only 16% percent of faculty groups actually work on establishing those goals. Teachers and principals spend most of their time planning and organizing.

All of us, health care workers included, would want health care groups to be high performance teams. However, based on the data I have collected, that is not often the case. Only 18% of health care groups function as high performance teams. We all need that percentage to increase significantly. I have consulted with health care groups in a number of hospital settings. Most of the hospital groups I encounter are in Stage 1 or 2. This may be due to a history of top-down patterns that have kept health care work groups in Stage 1 or 2 for generations. Changing those patterns is essential to the quality of patient care and important to health care workers.

Research conducted by my colleagues and me in 17 intensive care units established that fact. A total of 394 staff members of the intensive care units completed the Group Development Questionnaire. Each unit's predicted and actual mortality rates were calculated for the month in which data were collected. Hospital teams whose members and leaders worked together as high

Table 12.7   Health Care Work Groups at the Various Stage of
Development (N = 97)

STAGE 1 n = 21	22%	STAGE 2 n = 27	28%
STAGE 3 n = 32	32%	STAGE 4 n = 17	18%

performance teams saved more lives than hospital teams whose members and leaders did not. This was a very important study. I hope, for all of us, that all health care staffs become high performance teams. Health care teams can save so many more lives.

Do Leadership Teams or Membership Work Teams Function More Effectively?

Leadership teams consist of leaders and membership teams consist of members. In a research study that I conducted, the results suggested that membership teams and leadership teams have some similarities and some differences. The results of that study also suggested that leadership teams and membership teams, in general, are equally variable in terms of member perceptions of their internal dynamics. In some ways, this is good news. Not all leadership teams are inevitably trapped in patterns of unproductive dynamics. Many leadership teams are capable of functioning in productive ways. That is true of work teams as well.

Table 12.8   Percentages of Leadership and Membership Teams at the Different Stages of Development

	Stage 1	Stage 2	Stage 3	Stage 4
Leadership Teams	25%	35%	40%	0%
Work Teams	24%	25%	28%	23%

However, based on the evidence, a sizable percentage of leadership teams may not be able to function well. Sixty percent of the leadership teams were in Stage 1 and 2, and 40% of the leadership teams were in Stage 3. There were no leadership teams in Stage 4. In comparison, 49% of membership teams were in Stages 1 and 2, and 51% were in Stages 3 and 4. Given that research studies have determined that there is a link between the stage of group development and productivity, one can assume that a large percentage of leadership teams are not working as effectively or productively as they might.

A Final Thought

I hope that this fifth edition is useful and helpful for all the members and leaders of work groups out there. All of you are the real heroes of the 21st century. Individual heroism is a fine thing, but we need heroic work teams as well. Any time you hear of a scientific advancement, a newly created medicine, or a school where student achievement has improved significantly, a heroic team was behind it.

Thanks!

REFERENCES

Ale Ebrahim, N., Ahmed, S., & Taha, Z. (2009). Virtual teams: A literature review. *Australian Journal of Basic and Applied Sciences, 3*(3), 2653–2669.

Guzzo, R. A., Jett, R. D., & Katzell, R. A. (1985). The effects of psychologically-based intervention programs on worker productivity: A meta-analysis. *Personnel Psychology, 38,* 275–291.

Powell, A., Piccoli, G., & Ives, B. (2004). Virtual teams: A review of current literature and directions for future research. *Data Base for Advances in Information Systems, 35,* 6–39.

Schein, E. H. (1988). *Process consultation* (Rev. ed.). Reading, MA: Addison-Wesley.

Shaw, M. E. (1954). Some effects of problem complexity upon problem solution efficiency in different communication nets. *Journal of Experimental Psychology, 48,* 211–217.

Sundstrom, E., DeMeuse, K. P., & Futrell, D. (1990). Work teams: Applications and effectiveness. *American Psychologist, 45*(2), 120–133.

BIBLIOGRAPHY

———◆◆———

This bibliography is divided into the following 11 sections: groups and group development; virtual teams, groups and productivity; organizational culture; effective group membership; effective leadership; diversity in work teams, effective meetings; group processes and structures; team building, organizational development, and staff development; and team compensation.

Groups and Group Development

Akrivou, K., Boyatzis, R. E., & McLeod, P. L. (2006). The evolving group: Towards a prescriptive theory of intentional development. *Journal of Management Development, 25*(7), 689–706.

Arrow, H., Poole, M. S., Bouas Henry, K., Wheelan, S., & Moreland, R. (2004). Time, change and development: The temporal perspectives on groups. *Small Group Research, 35,* 73–105.

Bennis, W., & Shepard, H. (1956). A theory of group development. *Human Relations, 9,* 415–437.

Bion, W. (1961). *Experiences in groups.* New York, NY: Basic Books.

Burnand, G. (1990). Group development phases as working through six fundamental human problems. *Small Group Research, 21,* 255–273.

Bushe, G. R., & Coetzer, G. H. (2007). Group development and team effectiveness: Using cognitive representations to measure group development and predict task performance and group viability. *Journal of Applied Behavioral Science, 43*(2), 184–212.

Caple, R. (1978). The sequential stages of group development. *Small Group Behavior, 9,* 470–476.

Devine, D. J., Clayton, L. D., Philips, J. L., Dunford, B. B., & Melner, S. B. (1999). Teams in organizations: Prevalence, characteristics, and effectiveness. *Small Group Research, 30,* 678–711.

Gordon, J. (1992). Work teams: How far have they come? *Training, 29,* 59–65.

Hogan, R. (1975). Theoretical egocentrism and the problem of compliance. *American Psychologist, 30,* 533–539.

Mills, T. (1964). *Group transformations: An analysis of a learning group.* Englewood Cliffs, NJ: Prentice Hall.

Slater, P. (1966*). Microcosm.* New York, NY: Wiley.

Tilin, F., & Broder, J. (2005). Team consultation. In S. A. Wheelan (Ed.), *The handbook of group research and practice* (pp. 427–439). Thousand Oaks, CA: Sage.

Tuckman, B. W. (1965). Developmental sequence in small groups. *Psychological Bulletin, 63*(6), 384–399.

Tuckman, B. W., & Jensen, M. A. C. (1977). Stages in small group development revisited. *Group and Organizational Studies, 2,* 419–427.

Verdi, A. F., & Wheelan, S. (1992). Developmental patterns in same-sex and mixed-sex groups. *Small Group Research, 23*(3), 256–278.

Wheelan, S. (2004). Workplace teams. In J. L. DeLucia-Waack, D. A. Gerrity, C. R. Kalodner, & M. T. Riva (Eds.), *Handbook of group work* (pp. 401–413). Thousand Oaks, CA: Sage.

Wheelan, S. (2005). *Faculty groups: From frustration to collaboration.* Thousand Oaks, CA: Sage.

Wheelan. S. (2005). *Group processes: A developmental perspective* (2nd ed.). Boston, MA: Allyn & Bacon.

Wheelan, S. (2005). *Handbook of group research and practice.* Thousand Oaks, CA: Sage.

Wheelan, S., Davidson, B., & Tilin, F. (2003). Group development: Reality or illusion? *Small Group Research, 34,* 223–245.

Wheelan, S., & McKeage, R. (1993). Developmental patterns in small and large groups. *Small Group Research, 24*(1), 60–83.

Wheelan, S., & Verdi, A. (1992). Differences in male and female patterns of communication in groups: A methodological artifact? *Sex Roles: A Journal of Research, 27*(1/2), 1–15.

Wheelan, S., Verdi, A., & McKeage, R. (1994). *The group development observation system: Origins and applications.* Philadelphia, PA: P.E.P. Press.

Wheelan, S., & Williams, T. (2003). Mapping dynamic interaction patterns in work groups. *Small Group Research, 34,* 443–467.

Virtual Teams

Ahuja, M. K., & Carley, K. M. (1999). Network structure in virtual organizations. *Organization Science, 10,* 741–757.

Anawati, D., & Craig, A. (2006). Behavioral adaptation within cross-cultural virtual teams. *IEEE Transactions on Professional Communication, 49*(1), 44–56.

Andres, H. P. (2002). A comparison of face-to-face and virtual software development teams. *Team Performance Management, 8*(1/2), 39–48.

Archer, N. P. (1990). A comparison of computer conferences with face-to-face meetings for small group comparison of computer conferences with face-to-face meetings for small group business decisions. *Behaviour and Information Technology, 9,* 307–317.

Axelsson, K. (2003). Analysing business interaction in a virtual organization: Using business action theory to study complex inter-organisational contexts. *Journal of Electronic Commerce in Organizations, 1,* 1–27.

Balthazard, P., Potter, R. E., & Warren, J. (2004). Expertise, extraversion and group interaction styles as performance indicators in virtual teams. *Data Base for Advances in Information Systems, 35,* 41–64.

Black, L. W., Welser, H. T., Cosley, D., & DeGroot, J. M. (2011). Self-governance through group discussion in Wikipedia: Measuring deliberation in online groups. *Small Group Research, 42*(5), 595–634.

Chidambaram, L. (1996). Relational development in computer-supported groups. *MIS Quarterly, 20,* 143, 163.

D'Urso, S. C. (2009). The past, present, and future of human communication and technology research: An introduction. *Journal of Computer-Mediated Communication, 14,* 708–713.

Ale Ebrahim, N., Ahmed, S., & Taha, Z. (2009). Virtual teams: A literature review. *Australian Journal of Basic and Applied Sciences, 3*(3), 2653–2669.

Fiol, C., & O'Connor, E. (2005). Identification in face-to-face hybrid, and pure virtual teams: Untangling the contradictions. *Organization Science, 16*(1), 19–32.

Hardin, A. M., Fuller, M. A., & Valacich, J. S. (2006). Measuring group efficacy in virtual teams: New questions in an old debate. *Small Group Research, 37,* 65–85.

Krumpel, K. (2000). Making the right interactive moves for knowledge-producing tasks in computer-mediated groups. *IEEE Transactions on Professional Communication, 43,* 185–195.

Lind, M. R. (1999). The gender impact of temporary virtual work groups. *IEEE Transactions on Professional Communication, 42,* 276–285.

Majchrzak, A., Rice, R., Malhotra, A., King, N., & Ba, S. (2000). Technology adaptation: The case of a computer-supported inter-organizational virtual team. *MIS Quarterly, 24,* 569–600.

Maznevski, M. L., & Chudoba, K. M. (2000). Bridging space over time: Global virtual team dynamics and effectiveness. *Organization Science, 11*(5), 473–492.

Paul, S., Seetharaman, P., Samarah, I., & Mykytyn, P. P. (2004). Impact of heterogeneity and collaborative conflict management style on the performance of synchronous global virtual teams. *Information and Management, 41,* 303–321.

Rutkowski, A., Vogel, D., van Genuchten, M., & Saunders, C. (2008). Communication in virtual teams: Ten years of experience in education. *IEEE Transactions on Professional Communication, 51*(3), 302–312.

Sia, C. L., Tan, B. C. Y., & Wei, K.-K. (2002). Group polarization and computer-mediated communication: Effects of communication cues, social presence and anonymity. *Information Systems Research, 13,* 70–90.

Schiller, S. Z., & Mandviwalla, M. (2007). Virtual team research: An analysis of theory use and a framework for theory appropriation. *Small Group Research, 38*(12), 12–59.

Groups and Productivity

Bachiochi, P. D., Rogelberg, S. G., O'Connor, M. S., & Elder, A. E. (2000). The qualities of an effective team leader. *Organization Development Journal, 18*(1), 11–26.

Bruner, D. Y., & Greenlee, B. J. (2000). Measures of work culture in high and low performing schools. *Research in the Schools, 7*(2), 71–76.

Bushe, G. R. (2007). Group development and team effectiveness: Using cognitive representations to measure group development and predict task performance and group viability. *Journal of Applied Behavioral Science, 43*(2), 184–212.

Campany, N., Dubinsky, R., Urch Druskat, V., Mangino, M., & Flynn, E. (2007). What makes good teams work better: Research-based strategies that distinguish top-performing cross-functional drug development teams. *Organizational Development Journal, 25*(2), 179–186.

Evans, C. R., & Dion, K. L. (1991). Group cohesion and performance: A meta-analysis. *Small Group Research, 22*(2), 175–186.

Flowers, N., Mertens, S. B., & Mulhull, P. F. (1999). The impact of teaming: Five research-based outcomes. *Middle School Journal, 31*(2), 57–60.

Greene, C. N. (1989). Cohesion and productivity in work groups. *Small Group Behavior, 20,* 70–86.

Guzzo, R. A. (1990). Productivity research: Reviewing psychological and economic perspectives. In J. P. Campbell, R. J. Campbell, & Associates (Eds.), *Productivity in organizations* (pp. 63–81). San Francisco, CA: Jossey-Bass.

Hackman, J. R. (1990). *Groups that work (and those that don't).* San Francisco, CA: Jossey-Bass.

Hoy, K., & Hannum, J. W. (1997). Middle school climate: An empirical assessment of organizational health and student achievement. *Educational Administration Quarterly, 33*(3), 290–311.

Larson, C. E., & LaFasto, F. M. J. (1989). *Team work: What must go right/What can go wrong.* Newbury Park, CA: Sage.

Pritchard, R. D., Jones, S., Roth, P., Stuebing, K., & Ekeberg, S. (1988). Effects of group feedback, goal setting, and incentives on organizational productivity. *Journal of Applied Psychology, 73*(2), 337–358.

Reich, R. B. (1987). Entrepreneurship reconsidered: The team as hero. *Harvard Business Review, 64*(3), 77–83.

Shea, G. P., & Guzzo, R. A. (1987). Group effectiveness: What really matters? *Sloan Management Review, 3,* 25–31.

Shea, G. P., & Guzzo, R. A. (1987). Groups as human resources. In K. M. Rowland & G. R. Ferris (Eds.), *Research in personnel and human resources management* (Vol. 5, pp. 323–356). Greenwich, CT: JAI Press.

Sundstrom, E., DeMeuse, K. P., & Futrell, D. (1990). Work teams: Applications and effectiveness. *American Psychologist, 45*(2), 120–133.

Wheelan, S., & Brewer Danganan, N. (2003). The relationship between the internal dynamics of student affairs leadership teams and campus leaders' perceptions of the effectiveness of student affairs divisions. *National Association of Student Personnel Administrators Journal, 40*(3), 93–112.

Wheelan, S. (2009). Group size, group development and group productivity. *Small Group Research, 40*(2), 247–266.

Wheelan, S., & Burchill, C. (1999, April). Take teamwork to new heights. *Nursing Management,* pp. 28–32.

Wheelan, S., Burchill, C., & Tilin, F. (2003). The link between teamwork and patients' outcomes in intensive care units. *American Journal of Critical Care, 12,* 527–534.

Wheelan, S., & Kesselring, J. (2005). The link between faculty group development and the performance of elementary students on standardized tests. *Journal of Educational Research, 98,* 323–330.

Wheelan, S., & Lisk, A. (2000). Cohort group effectiveness and the educational achievement of adult undergraduate students. *Small Group Research, 31*(6), 724–738.

Wheelan, S., Murphy, D., Tsumura, E., & Fried-Kline, S. (1998). Member perceptions of internal group dynamics and productivity. *Small Group Research, 29*(3), 371–393.

Wheelan, S., & Tilin, F. (1999). The relationship between faculty group effectiveness and school productivity. *Small Group Research, 30*(1), 59–81.

Wheelan, S., Tillin, F., & Sanford, J. (1996). School group effectiveness and productivity. *Research Practice, 4*(1), 11–14.

Organizational Culture

Ancona, D. G. (1987). Groups in organizations: Extending laboratory models. In C. Hendrick (Ed.), *Group and intergroup processes* (pp. 207–230). Newbury Park, CA: Sage.

Cohen, M. D., & Sproull, L. S. (Eds.). (1996). *Organizational learning.* Thousand Oaks, CA: Sage.

Deal, T., & Peterson, K. (1999). *Shaping school culture: The heart of leadership.* San Francisco, CA: Jossey-Bass.

Deutsch, M. (1990). Forms of social organization: Psychological consequences. In H. T. Himmelweit & G. Gaskell (Eds.), *Societal psychology* (pp. 157–176). Newbury Park, CA: Sage.

Kennedy, F. A., Loughry, M. L., Klammer, T. P., & Beyerlein, M. M. (2009). Effects of organizational support on potency in work teams: The mediating role of team processes. *Small Group Research, 40*(1), 72–93.

O'Neil, J. (1995). On schools as learning organizations: A conversation with Peter Senge. *Educational Leadership, 52*(7), 20–23.

Schein, E. H. (1980). *Organizational psychology* (3rd ed.). Englewood Cliffs, NJ: Prentice Hall.

Schein, E. H. (1990). Organizational culture. *American Psychologist, 45*(2), 109–119.

Schein, E. (1991). What is culture? In P. J. Frost, L. F. Moore, M. R. Louis, C. C. Lundberg, & J. Martin (Eds.), *Reframing organizational culture* (pp. 243–253). Newbury Park, CA: Sage.

Tjosvold, D. (1991). *The conflict-positive organization: Stimulate diversity and create unity.* Reading, MA: Addison-Wesley.

Tjosvold, D., Dann, V., & Wong, C. (1992). Managing conflict between departments to serve customers. *Human Relations, 45,* 1035–1054.

Walton, R. E. (1985). From control to commitment in the workplace. *Harvard Business Review, 63*(2), 76–84.

Wheelan, S., & Abraham, M. (1993). The concept of intergroup mirroring: Reality or illusion? *Human Relations, 46*(7), 803–825.

Wheelan, S., & Conway, C. (1991). Group development as a framework to understand and promote school readiness to engage in an OD project. *Journal of Educational and Psychological Consultation, 2*(1), 59–71.

Wheelan, S., & Krasick, C. (1993). The emergence, transmission and acceptance of themes in a temporary organization. *Group and Organization Management, 18*(2), 237–260.

Effective Group Membership

Allen, M., & Bourhis, J. (1996). The relationship of communication apprehension to communication behavior: A meta-analysis. *Communication Quarterly, 44,* 214–226.

Bass, B. M., Wurster, C. R., Doll, P. A., & Clair, D. J. (1953). Situational and personality factors in leadership among sorority women. *Psychological Monographs, 67,* 16.

Belbin, R. (2010). *Team roles at work* (2nd ed.). Burlington, MA: Butterworth Heinmann/Elsevier.

Buck, R., Miller, R. E., & Caul, W. F. (1974). Sex, personality, and physiological variables in the communication of affect via facial expression. *Journal of Personality and Social Psychology, 30,* 587–596.

Haythorn, W. (1953). The influence of individual members on the characteristics of small groups. *Journal of Abnormal and Social Psychology, 48,* 276–284.

Karau, S. J., & Williams, K. D. (1993). Social loafing: A meta-analytic review and theoretical integration. *Journal of Personality and Social Psychology, 65,* 681–706.

Kogan, N., & Wallach, M. A. (1967). Group risk taking as a function of members' anxiety and defensiveness. *Journal of Personality, 35,* 50–63.

Leonard, R. L., Jr. (1975). Self-concept and attraction for similar and dissimilar others. *Journal of Personality and Social Psychology, 31,* 926–929.

McCroskey, J. C., Hamilton, P. R., & Weiner, A. N. (1974). The effect of interaction behavior on source credibility, homophily, and interpersonal attraction. *Human Communication Research, 1,* 42–52.

Ryan, E. D., & Lakie, W. L. (1965). Competitive and noncompetitive performance in relation to achievement motive and manifest anxiety. *Journal of Personality and Social Psychology, 1,* 342–345.

Sorrentino, R. M., & Sheppard, B. H. (1978). Effects of affiliation-related motives on swimmers in individual versus group competition: A field experiment. *Journal of Personality and Social Psychology, 36,* 704–714.

Teichman, Y. (1974). Predisposition for anxiety and affiliation. *Journal of Personality and Social Psychology, 29,* 405–410.

Effective Leadership

Angus-Leppan, T., Metcalf, L., & Benn, S. (2010). Leadership styles and CSR practice: An examination of sensemaking, institutional drivers and CSR leadership. *Journal of Business Ethics, 93,*189–213.

Avolio, B. (2007). Promoting more integrative strategies for leadership theory building. *American Psychologist, 62,* 25–33.

Bang, H., & Midelfart, T. N. (2008). Dialogue and effectiveness in management teams. *Tidsskrift for Norsk Psykologforening, 47,* 1.

Bang, H. (2012). What prevents senior executives from commenting upon miscommunication in top management team meetings? *Qualitative Research in Organizations and Management: An International Journal, 2,* 189–221.

Boyatzis, R., & McKee, A. (2005). *Resonant leadership.* Boston, MA: Harvard Business School Press.

Burke, W. W. (1986). Leadership as empowering others. In S. Srivasta & Associates (Eds.), *Executive power: How executives influence people and organizations* (pp. 51–77). San Francisco, CA: Jossey-Bass.

Conger, T. A., & Kanugo, R. N. (1988). *Charismatic leadership: The elusive factor in organizational effectiveness.* San Francisco, CA: Jossey-Bass.

DeRue, D. S., Barnes, C. M., & Morgeson, F. P. (2010). Understanding the motivational contingencies of team leadership. *Small Group Research, 41,* 621–651.

Goleman, D. (2011). *Leadership: The power of positive emotional intelligence.* Northhampton, MA: More Than Sound.

Dutton, J. E., Dukerich, J. M., & Harquail, C. V. (1994). Organizational images and member identification. *Administrative Science Quarterly, 39,* 239–263.

Hackman, J. R. (2002). *Leading teams: Setting the stage for great performances.* Boston, MA: Harvard Business School Press.

Hart, A. (1990). Managing school performance: The role of the administrator. In P. Reyes (Ed.), *Teachers and their workplace: Commitment, performance and productivity* (pp. 277–298). Newbury Park, CA: Sage.

Haslam, S. A., McGarty, C., Brown, P. M., Eggins, R. A., Morrison, B. E., & Reynolds, K. J. (1998). Inspecting the emperor's clothes: Evidence that random selection of leaders can enhance group performance. *Group Dynamics, 2,* 168–184.

Hershey, P., & Blanchard, K. H. (1976). Leader effectiveness and adaptability description (LEAD). In J. W. Pfeiffer & J. E. Jones (Eds.), *The 1976 annual handbook for group facilitators* (Vol. 5, pp. 68–79). La Jolla, CA: University Associates.

Hershey, P., & Blanchard, K. H. (1982). *Management of organizational behavior: Utilizing human resources* (4th ed.). Englewood Cliffs, NJ: Prentice Hall.

Hollander, E. P. (1995). Organizational leadership and followership. In P. Collett & A. Furnam (Eds.), *Social psychology at work* (pp. 69–87). London: Routledge.

Lumsden, G., & Lumsden, D. (1993). *Communicating in groups and teams: Sharing leadership.* Belmont, CA: Wadsworth.

Morgeson, F. P., & DeRue, D. S. (2010). Leadership in teams: A functional approach to understanding leadership structures and processes. *Journal of Management, 36*(1), 5–39.

Nicholls, J. R. (1985). A new approach to situational leadership. *Leadership and Organizational Development Journal, 6*(4), 2–7.

Northhouse, P. (2010). *Leadership: Theory and practice.* Thousand Oaks, CA: Sage.

Srivastava, A., Bartol, K. M., & Locke, E. A. (2006). Empowering leadership in management teams: Effects on knowledge sharing, efficacy and performance. *Academy of Management Journal, 49*(6), 1239–1251.

Turner, J. C., Oakes, P. J., Haslam, S. A., & McGarty, C. A. (1994). Self and collective: Cognition and social context. *Personality and Social Psychology Bulletin, 20,* 454–463.

Vecchio, R. P. (1987). Situational leadership theory: An examination of a prescriptive theory. *Journal of Applied Psychology, 72,* 444–451.

Von Cranach, M. (1986). Leadership as a function of group action. In C. F. Graumann & S. Moscovici (Eds.), *Changing conceptions of leadership* (pp. 115–134). New York, NY: Springer Verlag.

Vroom, V. H., & Jago, A. G. (1978). On the validity of the Vroom/Yetton model. *Journal of Applied Psychology, 63,* 151–162.

Vroom, V. H., & Yetton, P. W. (1973). *Leadership and decision-making.* Pittsburgh, PA: University of Pittsburgh Press.

Weiss, D., Tilin, F., & Morgan, M. (2013). *The interprofessional health care team: Leadership and development.* Burlington, MA: Jones & Bartlett Learning.

Wheelan, S. (2003). An initial exploration of the internal dynamics of leadership teams. *Consulting Psychology Journal, 55*(3), 179–188.

Diversity in Work Teams

Brief, A. P. (2008). *Diversity at work.* New York, NY: Cambridge University Press.

Ely, R. J., & Roberts, L. M. (2008). Shifting frames in team-diversity research: From difference to relationships. In A. P. Brief (Ed.), *Diversity at work* (pp. 175–201). New York, NY: Cambridge University Press.

Ely, R. J., & Thomas, D. A. (2001). Cultural diversity at work: The effects of diversity perspectives on work group processes and outcomes. *Administrative Science Quarterly, 46*(2), 229–273.

Jackson, S. E., Joshi, A., & Erhardt, N. L. (2003). Recent research on team and organizational diversity, SWOT analysis and implications. *Journal of Management, 29,* 801–830.

Jehn, K. A. (1995). A multi-method examination of the benefits and detriments of intragroup conflict. *Administrative Science Quarterly, 40,* 256–282.

Jehn, K. A., Greer, L. L., & Rupert, J. (2008). Diversity, conflict, and their consequences. In A. P. Brief (Ed.), *Diversity at work* (pp. 127–174). New York, NY: Cambridge University Press.

Kirchler, E., & Davis, J. H. (1986). The influence of member status differences and task type on group consensus and member position change. *Journal of Personality and Social Psychology, 51,* 83–91.

Knippenberg, D., & Schippers, M. (2007). Work group diversity. *Annual Review of Psychology, 58,* 515–541.

Lockheed, E., & Hall, K. (1976). Conceptualizing sex as a status characteristic: Applications to leadership training strategies. *Journal of Social Issues, 32,* 111–124.

Mannix, E. A., & Neale, M. A. (2005). What differences make a difference? The promise and reality of diverse teams in organizations. *Psychological Science in the Public Interest, 6*(2), 32–55.

Page, S. E. (2007). *The difference.* Princeton, NJ: Princeton University Press.

Wheelan, S. (1996). Effects of gender composition and group status differences on member perceptions of group developmental patterns, effectiveness, and productivity. *Sex Roles, 34*(9/10), 665–686.

Effective Meetings

Poole, M. S. (1991). Procedures for managing meetings: Social and technological innovation. In R. A. Swanson & B. O. Knapp (Eds.), *Innovative meeting management* (pp. 53–110). Austin, TX: 3M Meeting Management Institute.

Shelton, M. M., & Bauer, L. K. (1994). *Secrets of highly effective meetings.* Thousand Oaks, CA: Corwin.

Silberman, S. (1999). *101 ways to make meetings active: Surefire ideas to engage your group.* New York, NY: Wiley.

Tropman, J. E. (2003). *Making meetings work: Achieving high quality group decisions.* Thousand Oaks, CA: Corwin.

Group Processes and Structures

Amason, A. C., & Schweiger, D. M. (1994). Resolving the paradox of conflict, strategic decision making, and organizational performance. *International Journal of Conflict Management, 5,* 239–253.

Argote, L., Gruenfeld, D., & Naquin, C. (2001). Group learning in organizations. In M. E. Turner (Ed.), *Groups at work: Advances in theory and research* (pp. 369–411). Mahwah, NJ: Lawrence Erlbaum.

Barr, S. H., & Conlon, E. J. (1994). Effects of distribution of feedback in work groups. *Academy of Management Journal, 37*(3), 641–655.

Bunderson, J. S., & Sutcliffe, K. (2002). Comparing alternative conceptualizations of functional diversity in management teams: Process and performance effects. *Academy of Management Journal, 45,* 875–893.

Carnevale, P. J. D. (1986). Mediating disputes and decisions in organizations. In R. J. Lewicki, B. H. Sheppard, & M. H. Bazerman (Eds.), *Research on negotiation in organizations* (Vol. 1, pp. 251–269). Greenwich, CT: JAI Press.

Deutsch, M. (1971). Toward an understanding of conflict. *International Journal of Group Tensions, 1,* 42–54.

Deutsch, M. (1990). Cooperation, conflict and justice. In S. Wheelan, E. Pepitone, & V. Abt (Eds.), *Advances in field theory* (pp. 149–164). Newbury Park, CA: Sage.

Fisher, C. D., & Gitelson, R. (1983). A meta-analysis of the correlates of role conflict and ambiguity. *Journal of Applied Psychology, 68,* 320–333.

Gabarro, J. J. (1987). The development of working relationships. In J. W. Lorsch (Ed.), *Handbook of organizational behavior* (pp. 172–189). Englewood Cliffs, NJ: Prentice Hall.

Glynn, M. A., & Barr, P. S. (2003). Team decision making in organizations. In M. A. West, D. Tjosvold, & K. G. Smith (Eds.), *International handbook of organizational teamwork and cooperative learning* (pp. 211–228). New York, NY: Wiley.

Gratwitch, M. J., Munz, D. C., Elliott, E. K., & Mathis, A. (2003). Promoting creativity in temporary problem-solving groups: The effects of positive mood and autonomy in problem definition on idea-generating performance. *Group Dynamics, 7,* 200–213.

Hembroff, L. A. (1982). Resolving status inconsistency: An expectation states theory and test. *Social Forces, 61,* 183–205.

Hembroff, L. A., & Myers, D. E. (1984). Status characteristics: Degrees of task relevance and decision process. *Social Psychology Quarterly, 47,* 337–346.

Kemery, E. R., Bedeian, A. G., Mossholder, K. W., & Touliatos, J. (1985). Outcomes of role stress: A multisample constructive replication. *Academy of Management Review, 28,* 103–110.

Keyton, J. (1999). Relational communication in groups. In L. R. Frey, D. S. Gouran, & M. S. Poole (Eds.), *The handbook of group communication theory and research* (pp. 251–287). Thousand Oaks, CA: Sage.

Lovelace, K., Shapiro, D., & Weingart, L. R. (2001). Maximizing cross-functional new product teams' innovativeness and constraint adherence: A conflict communications perspective. *Academy of Management Journal, 24,* 779–784.

Miller, C. E., Jackson, P., Mueller, J., & Schersching, C. (1987). Some social psychological effects of group decision rules. *Journal of Personality and Social Psychology, 52,* 325–332.

Miller, C. E., & Wong, J. (1986). Coalition behavior: Effects of earned versus unearned resources. *Organizational Behavior and Human Decision Processes, 38,* 57–277.

Morris, W. N., & Miller, R. S. (1975). The effects of consensus-breaking and consensus pre-empting partners on reduction of conformity. *Journal of Experimental Social Psychology, 11,* 215–223.

Moscovici, S. (1985). Innovation and minority influence. In S. Moscovici, G. Mugny, & E. V. Avermate (Eds.), *Perspectives on minority influence* (pp. 9–48). Cambridge, UK: Cambridge University Press.

Moscovici, S. (1985). Social influence and conformity. In G. Lindzey & E. Aronson (Eds.), *Handbook of social psychology* (3rd ed., Vol. 1, pp. 347–412). New York, NY: Random House.

Nadler, D. A. (1979). The effects of feedback on task group behaviors: A review of the experimental research. *Organizational Behavior and Human Performance, 23,* 309–338.

Nadler, D. A., Cammann, C. T., & Mirvis, P. H. (1980). Developing a feedback system for work units: Field experiment in structural change. *Journal of Applied Behavioral Science, 16*(1), 41–62.

Peele, H. E. (2006). Appreciative inquiry and creative problem solving in cross-functional teams. *Journal of Applied Behavioral Science, 42*(4), 447–467.

Pruitt, D. G. (1987). Creative approaches to negotiation. In D. J. D. Sandole & I. Sandole-Staroste (Eds.), *Conflict management and problem solving: Interpersonal to international applications* (pp. 62–76). London, UK: Frances Pinter.

Pruitt, D. G., & Carnevale, P. J. D. (1992). The development of integrative agreements. In V. J. Derlega & J. Grezlak (Eds.), *Cooperative and helping behavior* (pp. 151–181). New York, NY: Academic Press.

Rawlins, W. K. (1984). Consensus in decision-making groups: A conceptual history. In G. M. Phillips & J. T. Wood (Eds.), *Emergent issues in human decision-making* (pp. 19–39). Carbondale: Southern Illinois University Press.

Salazar, A. J., Hirokawa, R. Y., Propp, K. M., Julian, K. M., & Leatham, G. B. (1994). In search of true causes: Examination of the effect of group potential and group interaction on decision performance. *Human Communication Research, 20,* 529–559.

Shaw, M. E. (1954). Some effects of problem complexity upon problem solution efficiency in different communication nets. *Journal of Experimental Psychology, 48,* 211–217.

Stewart, G. L. (2006). A meta-analytic review of relationships between team design features and team performance. *Journal of Management, 32*(1), 29–54.

Sundstrom, E., & Altman, I. (1989). Physical environments and work group effectiveness. In L. L. Cummings & B. Staw (Eds.), *Research in organizational behavior* (Vol. 11, pp. 175–209). Greenwich, CT: JAI Press.

Theodorson, G. A. (1962). The function of hostility in small groups. *Journal of Social Psychology, 256,* 57–66.

Weldon, E., Jehn, K., & Pradhan, P. (1991). Processes that mediate the relationship between a group goal and improved group performance. *Journal of Personality and Social Psychology, 61*(4), 555–569.

Wheelan, S. (2009). Group size, group development and group productivity. *Small Group Research, 40*(2), 247–262.

Team Building, Organizational Development, and Staff Development

Buzaglo, G., & Wheelan, S. (1999). Facilitating work team effectiveness: Case studies from Central America. *Small Group Research, 30,* 108–129.

Cummings, T. G. (1981). Designing effective work-groups. In P. C. Nystrom & W. Starbuck (Eds.), *Handbook of organizational design* (Vol. 2, pp. 250–271). Oxford, UK: Oxford University Press.

Evans, N., & Jarvis, D. (1986). The group attitude scale: A measure of attraction to group. *Small Group Behavior, 17*(2), 203–216.

Goldstein, I. L. (Ed.). (1989). *Training and development in organizations.* San Francisco, CA: Jossey-Bass.

Guskey, T. R. (1988). Teacher efficacy, self-concept, and attitudes toward the implication of instructional innovation. *Teacher and Teacher Education, 4,* 63–69.

Guzzo, R. A., Jett, R. D., & Katzell, R. A. (1985). The effects of psychologically-based intervention programs on worker productivity: A meta-analysis. *Personnel Psychology, 38,* 275–291.

Joyce, B., & Showers, B. (1995). *Student achievement through staff development: Fundamentals of school renewal* (2nd ed.). New York, NY: Longman.

Salas, E., Rozell, D., Mullen, B., & Driskell, J. E. (1999). The effect of team building on performance: An integration. *Small Group Research, 30,* 309–329.

Schein, E. H. (1988). *Process consultation* (Rev. ed.). Reading, MA: Addison-Wesley.

Silberman, M. (1990). *Active training.* Lexington, MA: Lexington Books.

Tannenbaum, S. I., Beard, R. L., & Salas, E. (1992). Team building and its influence on team effectiveness: An examination of conceptual and empirical developments. In K. Kelley (Ed.), *Issues, theory, and research in industrial/organizational psychology* (pp. 117–153). Amsterdam: Elsevier.

Wheelan, S. (1990). *Facilitating training groups.* New York, NY: Praeger.

Wheelan, S., Brunner, A., Burchill, C., Craig, R., & Tilin, F. (1996). The utility of group development theory in consulting with small, social service organizations: A case study. *Organization Development Journal, 14*(3), 4–15.

Wheelan, S., Buzaglo, G., & Tsumura, E. (1998). Developing assessment tools for cross cultural group research. *Small Group Research, 29*(3), 359–370.

Wheelan, S., & Furber, S. (2006). Facilitating team development: Communication and productivity. In L. Frey (Ed.), *Facilitating group communication in context: Innovations and applications with natural groups* (Vol. 2, pp. 155–176). Thousand Oaks, CA: Sage.

Wheelan, S., & Hochberger, J. (1996). Validation studies of the Group Development Questionnaire. *Small Group Research, 27*(1), 143–170.

Team Compensation

Brown, M., & Heywood, J. S. (2002). *Paying for performance: An international comparison.* London, UK: M. E. Sharpe.

Caudron, S. (1994). Tie individual pay to team success. *Personnel Journal, 73*(19), 40–46.

Fehr, E., & Falk, A. (2002). Psychological foundations of incentives. *European Economic Review, 14,* 687–724.

Gross, S. E. (1995). *Compensation for teams: How to design and implement team-based reward systems.* New York, NY: American Management Association.

Hamilton, B., Nickerson, J., & Owan, H. (2003). Team incentives and worker heterogeneity: An empirical analysis of the impact of teams on productivity and participation. *Journal of Political Economy, 111,* 465–497.

Honeywell, J. A., Dickinson, A. M., & Poling, A. (1997). Individual performance as a function of individual and group pay contingencies. *Psychological Record, 47*(2), 261–274.

Kauhanen, A., & Piekkola, H. (2006). What makes performance-related pay schemes work? Finnish evidence. *Journal of Management Governance, 10,* 149–177.

Mohrman, S. A., Cohen, S. G., & Mohrman, A. M., Jr. (1995). *Designing team-based organizations: New forms of knowledge work.* San Francisco, CA: Jossey-Bass.

Parker, G., McAdams, J., & Zielinski, D. (2000). *Rewarding teams: Lessons from the trenches.* San Francisco, CA: Jossey-Bass.

Saunier, A. M., & Hawk, E. J. (1994). Realizing the potential of teams through team-based rewards. *Compensation and Benefits Review, 26*(4), 24–33.

Sherriton, J., & Stern, J. (1997). *Corporate culture/team culture: Removing the hidden barriers to team success.* New York, NY: American Management Association.

Zingheim, P. K., & Schuster, J. R. (1997). Best practices for small-team pay. *ACA Journal, 6*(1), 40–49.

INDEX

Ability-based choice of members, 13
Age of a group, and productivity, 132
Ahmed, S., 125
Ale Ebrahim, N., 125
Attendance, 35
Autonomy, 17

Beginning groups. *See* Stage 1 (dependency
    and inclusion)
Blaming, 50–53
Blogging, 128
Business work groups, 132–133

Checklists
    Effective Leader Checklist, 84–89
    Effective Member Checklist, 64–69
    Organizational Support Checklist, 18–23
    Team Performance Checklist,
        45–48, 122
Clarifying questions, 53–54
Coalitions
    factions, 78
    subgroups, 34–35, 104–106
Cohesion, 61–64, 119–120
Collaborative work, history of, 1–2
Communication
    conflict resolution and, 63–64
    discussion, 43, 58
    freedom of expression, 59
    open communication structure, 42, 54–56
    with other groups, 110–111
    ratio of task communications to supportive
        communications, 56
Compensation strategies, 10
Compromise, 33–34

Computer-mediated discourse, 125
Conflict
    blaming, patterns of, 50–53
    confrontational, 101–102
    diversity and, 59–60
    factions over leadership, 78
    high performance teams and conflict
        management, 45
    interpersonal, 26, 60
    personal feuds and personality
        conflicts, 33, 102
    personalizing vs. group perspective, 80
    as sign of progress, 32–33
    stage 2 and, 96–97, 98, 101–102
    stage 4 and, 119–120
    task conflicts, 26–27, 33, 45, 60
    third-party interventions in, 81
Conflict resolution
    leadership and, 81
    members and, 62–64
    methods of, 63
    stage 2 and, 106
Consensus, 58, 119
Continuous learning, 12
Cooperation, 45, 61–62, 64
Counterdependency and fighting stage.
    See Stage 2 (counterdependency
    and fighting)
Culture, organizational, 7–10
Culture of a group, 71, 96, 97–102

Decision making
    changing the process, 119
    high performance teams and, 43
    informal processes of, 104

large groups and, 131
member participation in, 56–59
methods for, 57
stage 2 and, 104
stage 4 and, 117–119
Defensiveness, 80
DeMeuse, K. P., 15
Dependency and inclusion stage. *See* Stage 1
    (dependency and inclusion)
Detail, paying attention to, 9, 117
Development. *See* Group development
Disagreements. *See* Conflict
Discussion, 43, 58, 94–95
Diversity
    conflicts and, 59–60
    individual behavioral differences, 43–44
    performance level and, 30
    status, open communication, and, 55

Education. *See* Training
Education work groups, 133–134
Effective Leader Checklist, 84–89
Effective Member Checklist, 64–69
Empowerment, 79
Evaluation
    group progress assessment, 35
    high performance teams and, 43, 121
    problem solving and, 58–59
    See also Checklists
Expectations, clear, 10
Expression, freedom of, 59
External environment, management of, 77

Face-to-face meetings vs. teleconferencing,
    13. *See also* Virtual teams
Facilitation by members, 82
Factions, 78
Feedback
    constructive, 42
    helping too much and, 16–17
    high performance teams and, 42
    internal and external, 42
    interventions and, 15
    positive, in stage 1, 75
    stage 4 and, 122–123
Feuds, personal, 33, 102
Fighting. *See* Conflict; Stage 2
    (counterdependency and fighting)
Freedom of expression, 59
Fundamental attribution error, 51
Futrell, D., 15

GDQ consultants, 125, 127–129
GDQ Online Scoring System, 128–129
Goals
    clarifying questions, 53–54
    conflict over, 98
    discussing and clarifying in stage 1, 94–95
    goal setting as intervention, 15
    high performance teams and, 38–39
    interdependence and, 40–41
    meaningful, 11–12
    of stage 1, 90
    of stage 2, 96–97
    of stage 3, 108
    of stage 4, 114–115
    success, expectation of, 8–9, 116–117
Group culture, 71, 96, 97–102
Group development
    adjusting leadership for, 73–74
    assessing progress, 35
    attendance, 35
    characteristics by stage, 25–30
    compromise and, 33–34
    concept of, 24
    conflict as sign of progress, 32–33
    diversity and, 30
    integrated model of, 24
    knowledge about, 31
    member responsibility, 34
    murky beginnings, 32
    patience with, 31–32
    personal feuds and personality conflicts
        and, 33
    subgroups and coalitions, 34–35
    supportiveness, 34
    survival tips, 30–35
    time frame for, 130
    timely task completion, 34
    uneven process of, 30
    See also Stage 1 (dependency
        and inclusion); Stage 2
        (counterdependency and fighting);
        Stage 3 (trust and structure); Stage
        4 (work)
Group Development Questionnaire (GDQ),
    125, 128–129, 134
Group members. *See* Members of groups
    and teams
Groups
    age of, 132
    dislike of working in, 2
    everyday need for, 1–2

as interdependent systems, 71, 72
knowledge base and, 2
size of, 131
See also Work groups
Groupthink, 62
Guzzo, R. A., 15

Health care work groups, 134–135
Helplessness, feelings of, 50–51
High performance teams
    characteristics of, 36–37
    communication and feedback in, 42
    conflict management and, 45
    cooperation in, 45
    decision making in, 117–119
    goals, clear, 38–39
    implementation and evaluation by, 43
    individual behavior differences in, 43–44
    interdependence and, 40–41
    leadership roles in, 41
    norms, establishing, 43
    norms for quality and high performance,
        115–116
    planning, decision making, and
        discussion in, 43
    roles in, 39–40
    structure and, 44–45
    Team Performance Checklist for,
        45–48, 122
    See also Stage 4 (work)
Human resources, access to, 12

Implementation, 43, 59
Inclusion concerns in stage 1, 91–92
Individual behavioral differences, 43–44
Individual performance vs. teamwork, 10
Innovation, 8, 60, 61, 116
Interdependence
    group goals and tasks and, 11
    groups as interdependent systems,
        71, 72
    high performance teams
        and, 40–41
Intervention strategies, 15–16
Introverts, 91 (box)
Ives, B., 125–126

Jett, R. D., 15

Katzell, R. A., 15
Knowledge base, group role in, 2

Labor, division of, 62, 105, 109
Leadership
    charismatic leaders, 70, 72
    conflict resolution and, 81
    confrontational challenges, 101–102
    Effective Leader Checklist, 84–89
    external environment, managing, 77
    facilitating group growth, 75–76
    group membership of a leader, 84
    high performance teams and, 41
    member facilitation, 82
    organizational support reviews and, 83
    overfocus on, 3
    parenting compared to, 74
    performance standards, setting, 77
    personalizing vs. group perspective
        and, 80
    positive feedback and, 75
    power and, 78–79
    progress and regression, monitoring, 83
    reducing member anxiety, fear, and
        concerns, 75
    stage 1 and, 74–77, 92–93
    stage 2 and, 77–81
    stage 3 and, 81–82, 109, 110
    stage 4 and, 83
    structural changes and, 82
    style adjustments, 73–74
    supervision, training, and education for
        members, 76–77
    training and, 14
    traits, skills, and selection of roles, 72–73
    views of, 70–72
Leadership teams vs. membership teams, 135
Learning, continuous, 12
The Learning Bridge, 129
LinkedIn, 127

Manufacturing work groups, 133
Membership teams vs. leadership teams, 135
Members of groups and teams
    ability-based choice of, 13
    blame patterns and, 50–53
    clarifying questions by, 53–54
    cohesion and cooperation, 61–64
    dependency, anxiety, and need for
        inclusion and safety, 75
    Effective Member Checklist, 64–69
    leadership involvement by, 82, 109, 110
    norms and, 60–61
    number of, 44

problem-solving and decision-making procedures, 56–59

ratio of task communications to supportive communications and, 56

status classifications, open communication structure, and, 54–56

supporting productivity, innovation, and free expression for, 59–60

training, lack of, 49–50

See also Conflict; Diversity; Training

Minorities. *See* Diversity

Mission of groups, 17

Mission statements, organizational, 8

Negotiation, 64, 81

Norms

decision making and, 119

high performance teams and, 43

productivity and, 60–61

for quality and high performance, 115–116

stage 2 and, 99–100

Number of members, 44

Open communication structure, 42, 54–56

Operational procedure reviews, 120

Organizational culture, 7–10

Organizational support

autonomy and connection, 17

checklist for, 18–23

favorable organizational culture, 7–10

giving groups what they need, 11–13

helping too much, 16–17

importance of, 7

intervention strategies, 15–16

review sessions on, 17–18, 83

training, trainers, and, 14–15

Organizational Support Checklist, 18–23

Performance standards, setting, 77

Personality conflicts, 33, 102

Piccoli, G., 125–126

Planning

detail awareness and, 9

education work groups and, 134

group age and, 132

high performance teams and, 43

lack of, 58

stage 1 and, 94, 95

strategic plans in high performance teams, 38–40

for structural changes, 82

Powell, A., 125–126

Power

redistribution of, 73, 79

types of, 78–79

Problem solving

conflict and, 63

diversity and, 60

member participation in, 56–59

methods for, 57

stage 4 and, 117–119

Productivity

group age and, 132

group size and, 131

high performance teams and, 45

internal team processes, relationship with, 36–37

keys to, 37–45

norms and, 60–61

process losses and routine in stage 4, 123–124

structure changes to facilitate, 82

Profit vs. quality and service, 9

Quality, 9, 115–116. *See also* High performance teams

Questions, clarifying, 53–54

Recognition, 10

Recommendations from teams, valuing, 9–10

Regression, 83, 122

Relationship building in stage 3, 111–113

Responsibility, taking, 34

Revitalization, 124

Roles

clarifying questions on, 53–54

dissatisfaction and clarification in stage 2, 102–103

in high performance teams, 39–40

leadership roles, selection of, 73

Routine, avoiding, 124

Safety concerns in stage 1, 91–92

Schein, E. H., 52

Service vs. profit, 9

Shaw, M. E., 57

Size of groups, 131

Skype, 127–128

Stage 1 (dependency and inclusion)

characteristics of, 25–26

goals of, 90

leader dependency, 92–93

leadership at, 74–77
leadership perceptions and, 41
order and structure, wish for, 93–95
safety and inclusion concerns, 91–92
time frame for, 130 (table)
Stage 2 (counterdependency and fighting)
characteristics of, 26–27
goals of, 96–97
leadership at, 77–81
leadership perceptions and, 41
time frame for, 130 (table)
unfed group structure, creating, 102–107
unified group culture, creating, 97–102
Stage 3 (trust and structure)
characteristics of, 27–28
fine-tuning of roles, organization, and
structure in, 108–111
goals of, 108
leadership at, 81–82, 109
leadership perceptions and, 41
relationship building in, 111–113
time frame for, 130 (table)
Stage 4 (work)
characteristics of, 28–30
cohesion and conflict in, 119–120
decision making and problem solving in,
117–119
getting the work done well, 115–117
goals of, 114–115
high performance, maintenance of,
121–124
leadership at, 83
leadership perceptions and, 41
time frame for, 130 (table)
Star Trek, 129
Status classifications, 54–56
Strategic plans, 38–40
Strategies for team development,
3–4, 15–16
Structure
change to facilitate productivity, 82
group size, 131
high performance teams and, 44–45
stage 1 and, 93–95
unified, in stage 2, 102–107
See also Roles; Stage 3 (trust and
structure)
Subgroups, 34–35, 104–106
Success, expectation of, 8–9, 116–117
Sundstrom, E., 15
Supervision, 76–77

Support from the organization. See
Organizational support
Supportive statements, 34, 56

Taha, Z., 125
Task clarification, 53–54
Task competence and leadership, 73
Task conflicts, 26–27, 33, 45, 60
Tasks, meaningful, 11–12
Team members. See Members of groups
and teams
Team Performance Checklist,
45–48, 122
Teams, high performance. See High
performance teams
Teams, virtual, 125–129
Teams vs. work groups, 2–3
Teamwork, 2, 3, 10
Technical resources, access to, 12
Teleconferencing vs. face-to-face
meetings, 13. See also
Virtual teams
Time for teams, sufficient, 44–45
Timely task completion, 34
Training
educating for group participation
competence, 14–15
leader focus, 3
membership training, lack
of, 49–50
stage 1 leadership and, 76–77
Trust
conflict resolution and, 64
stage 2 and, 105
stage 3 and, 112, 113
timely task completion and, 34
Trust and structure stage. See Stage 3
(trust and structure)

Video conferences, 126–127
Virtual teams, 125–129

Wheelan, Susan, xii
Work areas, defined, 13
Work groups
defined, 2
in different sectors, 132–135
history of, 1
teams and, 2–3
See also Group development
Work stage. See Stage 4 (work)

⑤SAGE researchmethods

The essential online tool for researchers from the world's leading methods publisher

Find exactly what you are looking for, from basic explanations to advanced discussion

More content and new features added this year!

"I have never really seen anything like this product before, and I think it is really valuable."

John Creswell, University of Nebraska–Lincoln

Discover **Methods Lists**—methods readings suggested by other users

Watch video interviews with leading methodologists

Explore the **Methods Map** to discover links between methods

Search a custom-designed taxonomy with more than 1,400 qualitative, quantitative, and mixed methods terms

Uncover more than 120,000 pages of book, journal, and reference content to support your learning

Find out more at
www.sageresearchmethods.com